ENDORSEMENTS

The Real Deal

Kelly Coray is the real deal. That's what you get in her powerful, personal account of facing challenges, struggling at times...but with each battle, overcoming. Dave and I have witnessed Kelly over the years redeem her life lessons to not only press on with greater strength, but to build up others as well. You can draw on her honest, conversational style to learn valuable insights and be encouraged. You will be challenged to apply the principles she has proven.

~ **Susan Wells / David Wells**,
General Superintendent, Pentecostal Assemblies of Canada

Practical, Conversational, Inspirational

Kelly seems like the kind of person I would like for a best friend. Not only because she's witty and insightful, but because she speaks truthfully. Reading this practical, conversational book was inspirational to me.

~ **Jeanne Halsey**,
Christian Writer (*The Story Behind Don Gossett's "My Never Again List"* ... *What's That You Have In Your Hands?* ... *The Parable of Aurelia*), Public Speaker; Birch Bay, Washington

I'VE GOT YOUR BAGGAGE...NOW FOLLOW ME

By **Kelly Coray**

I'VE GOT YOUR BAGGAGE... NOW FOLLOW ME
By **Kelly Coray**

ISBN 978-1-365-31995-2

I've Got Your Baggage...Now Follow Me, by Kelly Coray (1967); with Michael Gossett (1951~); copyright © 2016; published by *lulu Canada*; ISBN 978-1-365-31995-2. This book is protected under the Copyright Laws of the United States of America; all rights reserved under International Copyright Law. No part of this book may be reproduced or transmitted in any form or by any means, electronic or mechanical, including photocopying, recording, or by information storage and retrieval system in any manner whatsoever, without express advance written permission of the Author, except in the case of brief quotations embodied in critical articles and reviews.

Unless otherwise stated, all Scriptures quoted are taken from the **Holy Bible, New International Version** ® [NIV]; copyright © 1973, 1978, 1984, 2011 by Biblica, Inc.®; used by permission; all rights reserved worldwide. *The Message* [MSG] by Eugene H. Peterson; © 1993, 1994, 1995, 1996, 2000, 2001, 2002; published by Tyndale House Publishers, Carol Stream, Illinois, 60188; used by permission; all rights reserved worldwide.

All pictures are property of Kelly Coray
Photographer: Dareian Li Matsuda
Printed in Canada.

For more information, contact: jkcoray@shaw.ca

TABLE OF CONTENTS

Title Page..5
Dedication...9
Foreword..13
Introduction by Michael Gossett...................17
Chapter 1: The Discovery..........................19
Chapter 2: The Man in The Mirror...............31
Chapter 3: Being Heard............................45
Chapter 4: Lies, Suppression and Control....51
Chapter 5: Actions Do Speak Louder than Word...67
Chapter 6: Own It and Move On.................75
Chapter 7: Mindset, Unity and a Music Festival.
....83
Chapter 8: Purity....................................97
Chapter 9: Discovering the Truth...............117
Chapter 10: Authenticity and the Samaritan Woman..131
Chapter 11: Hearing from God...................151
Chapter 12: Thanks for the Memories.........173
Chapter 13: Testimony.............................191
Chapter 14: Peeling an Important Onion.....217
Chapter 15: Journey to the Finish Line.......239
Bibliography and Resources......................251

DEDICATION

Thank you to my incredibly loving and patient husband Jay, for hanging in there with me on this long process and journey to freedom. Only you and God know the agony I have battled in writing this book. You have been true to me, consistent and encouraging all throughout. You never stopped believing in me, and in us.

Natasha: you are such an unselfish encourager, you really model thoughtfulness as a woman. So intelligent, and always diligently willing to learn. You amaze me!

Kayla: your beautiful voice and your carefully expressed thoughts have lifted me many times. You have real compassion and are an exceptional listener, especially to your momma.

Shenae: you always know how to bless me with an encouraging text. The way you honour me and your Daddy is such a blessing. You are so sweet.

Colter: you seem to know when to serve and protect me, or give me a much-needed hug.

Jason: your mind is brilliant and you stretch me in our debates and challenges.

My amazing grandchildren.

Elijah: you are my hero, you are a fighter, a survivor and an over-comer. Great things are ahead for you, and I am proud of you.

Jarron: you are both a lover and a comedian. You are never too busy to give a hug or a kiss. You know how to make me laugh deep in my stomach!

Charleigh: brilliant ham, sweet ladybug, I am baffled with your wit, knowledge and sense of humor. You know when to make me laugh.

My mom, Marie: you are such a wise and caring woman of God who is always consistent in support and love. You are also practical and direct, and give me excellent advice, when I need that. Your continued help in the process of writing this book has been amazing. Thank you so much.

Klayton: Watching you with your family is such a delight. Dad would be so proud of you! I love you brother.

Jay's mom, Gwen: my second mother, you have been by balance. Consistent in love and knowledge. Thank you so much for keeping me grounded. You have taught me unconditional love.

My cousins but like brothers, Rene and Kent: thank you for a lifetime of love, laughter, support and protection. And their wives Patricia and Sara, You girls are the bomb. So much fun to be with, and you both have been a great support.

To all my friends and family: I wouldn't be who I am if it wasn't for your honesty and kindness along the way. Thank you all for your on going support and encouragement.

To the "rack pack" I have known since 1980: Thank you all so much for such a fun ride together. Stuck like glue...through thick and thin, I know I can depend on you, you are family. I love you all.

Donna: my greatest cheerleader and a true friend. You have protected me, and you have believed in me. You know me inside out and keep loving me.

Dan: my brother from another mother. You speak wisdom to me, like the true Pastor that you are.

Many others have touched my life, and I value you. Bless you all.

FORWARD
by, **Kelly Coray**

We are to go, tell, and be who Jesus has been to us. The world is full of troubles and despair, and so many are looking for hope, and a light in the darkness. Once upon a time I might have thought that I had to have it all together and be perfect before God could use me in a meaningful way. I learned something quite different about that.

I have gone through more than most, but I have overcome because I am a warrior. I have fought battles, I have fought demons, and I have led others to victory. My weapons in spiritual warfare are always ready to use. My discernment is sharp, my prayer never ceases, and my worship grounds me by reminding me whose I am.

Some of the places I have had to go have been frightening and even horrific, yet I have always had this steadying belief that Jesus was right there with me. He has never left me. Why? Because He loves me and has a magnificent plan for my life.

God is interested in being there in the process for us. It's really not about perfection. It is about simple faith in Him and obeying His voice. The Lord is not a fair-weather friend, rather He is often more present (if that is possible) in the troubles and the tribulations. I have long ago given up trying to figure out why God loves me and has called me. He does and He has. I follow. That's it.

Our weakness provides opportunity for the Lord to be the strength of our lives. Fear of others will keep us bound and impotent, but trust in God will liberate us. We know from the Bible that none of us are here by accident. Each of us is 'fearfully and wonderfully made', and part of our journey is to find out what God wants to do in us and through us. He will show us the way as we follow Him, and He loves to bless us with new challenges and opportunities.

This bad old world is all about narcissism: self promotion, self gratification and selfishness. Many ask the question: "Why do we need a Savior?"

Life is much more than just the 'here and now'. I believe in Eternity. Jesus Christ offers eternal life. It is one of the themes of this book.

I hope that you enjoy reading the story of my journey, and that you will laugh and cry with me. I have been candid. You will hear my heart, and my commitment to being authentic and open. I realize that being this way is a threat to some, and uncomfortable to others. I ask that you hear my heart, and join me.

Find your song. It may take a little longer than you might think, but I promise that it will be worth it. This book has taken nine years, and I believe that God's timing is perfect.

I pray that this book finds each reader at precisely the right time. I pray that this journey instills hope into you. You are highly valued and significant to God. He stands at the door knocking. Will you let Him in?

Kelly Coray

INTRODUCTION
by Michael Gossett

Please allow me to introduce you to an amazing storyteller, Kelly Coray. So, why would you want to take the time to read her story?

Human beings thrive on stories. If a good teacher wants to make a point stick, they will usually tell a great story. Communication between humans is vital but often it is not particularly effective. Turn on the TV, Radio or the Internet (or whatever) and you just may conclude that most talk is cheap and that words don't carry much value.

It doesn't have to be that way. The master storyteller, Jesus Christ, often used stories to sell his ideas. One life-changing story He told was about a Prodigal Son. Jesus knew that a well told story can make all the difference.

Kelly Coray is a lady with many communication talents: she sings, she leads, she speaks, she creates, she counsels and more. She is also an excellent storyteller. Her story is worth reading because it is fascinating, has surprises, and it also rings true. Most will find her story interesting while many will find her story profound and others may have their lives changed by Kelly's story.

That shouldn't really be a surprise to the reader, because you will soon understand that Kelly Coray knows the master storyteller very well.

Chapter 1: **The Discovery**

Before I formed you in the womb I knew you, before you were born I set you apart.
                                         Jeremiah 1:5a (NIV)

For What It's Worth

We have all asked that same question: *"How much is that worth?"* We want to know, because worth and value are more than just a price. Perhaps a better question to ask is: *"How much is she worth?"* or *"How much is he worth?"*

"Is she worth enough for me to be chosen?" Sometimes it is difficult to measure worth just by looking at the obvious, or the outside. Often we might just make a decision to choose, based purely on the outside, the *"outward appearance"* as the Bible states. Many do just that.

Remembering back during our school days, most of us had our entire class in our Physical Education Class. Girls, boys, athletes, sluggards, etc. (Pretty much all of the *Village People,* it seemed.) Often there were games that required two sides and that meant that two teams had to be chosen. The teacher would select two team leaders and the picking would begin.

Rarely would team leaders choose their friends because the goal was to win, so the most athletically inclined were picked up immediately. If it were a large class, then the next few moments became some of the hardest moments in our lives. Why? Worth and value were clearly determined by how quickly you were chosen.

Can you remember this? We all sat there quietly trying desperately to look cool, but inside we were almost yelling, *"Pick me! Pick me! Please!"* If we were less than gifted athletically, we knew what everybody knew: the most athletically challenged and the least popular children would be left standing alone, and on full display. These kids would receive a powerful social message of ridicule. It was clear, and everybody knew it.

I remember watching this happen to several kids in my class. In my still-developing heart, I had something of an understanding and empathy for some of these poor kids. While in that moment playing the game seemed like the most important thing, I was beginning to understand that worth is more than how adept one is with a ball or with a team, or which team happened to win that day.

That is not the end of the story, either. It's a fact that some of those poor kids may have experienced some early defeats, losses or embarrassments, and had some real struggles with self-worth. Yet many years later, at the high school reunion, some of those very same rejected, picked-on kids showed up having attained real success, feeling fulfilled and looking quite amazing. The rejects may have been laughed at, but in the end, they had the last laugh.

Life Is A Marathon

Should we be surprised? Not if we stop to think about it. Life is not a sprint – it is always a marathon. Those "stars" in elementary school (those first picked) were sprinters and they did quite well ... at the beginning. Some of the successful few former rejects were marathon runners – in it for the long haul. The marathon runners may not have had the same speed as the sprinters, but those kids had something the sprinters didn't have: they had endurance.

I will admit that it is more fun to watch a sprint. Things happen quickly because in the sprint, the race is pretty brief. (One of the challenges of this modern age we are living in, is that many things are compartmentalized into 30 or 60 minute increments.) This is very noticeable on television. For the most part, we don't seem to have a lot of patience for things that run longer. On the other hand, marathon runners are slow and steady, and frankly not as exciting. Sometimes it hardly seems like much of a race.

While athletes always have to train, I believe that ultimately, it is much more of a challenge to become a successful marathon runner in some ways, and yet more types of people can be successful at running marathons than the few just running sprints. (We call that irony.)

We have worth even when we are broken. God isn't expecting perfection in us. This is really good news! He decides to love us, to help us, and to choose us first. God hasn't missed anything ... He knows all about our past and our failures, but He has special plans for us and our future. Our Father is very deliberate about our lives, He already knows the beginning from the end, and His plans for you are good, and not bad.

News Flash: **God is not freaked out with us!** If we would only believe in ourselves as much as God does, I suspect that many of our lives would flow much more smoothly than they do currently. God put His part of things into place before we made any move toward Him at all. Here is something to consider: many of us don't really know much about ourselves, let alone our Heavenly Father. If you stick with me in this book, we should be able to help correct that situation, for a few of us anyway.

What Is Your Measuring Stick?

This business of worth, value and self-esteem has become a very complicated business. Why? Because we – as the human race – have made it that way. From an early age, many of us seem to equate worth with achievement, physical prowess or with beauty.

I won't be the first person to say that we have been sold a "bill of goods" by society in terms of the unhealthy, unbiblical preoccupation with physical beauty. Yet what is the constant, unrelenting message in much of the press? The beautiful, the young, the successful – these are the people to pay attention to, and to follow. You need to look younger, slimmer, sexier, and more desirable than you actually are because it is all about image. You can be 50 or 60, but you will do better in this society if you look like you are 20 or 30. There are several messages here: *"You gotta look young, you gotta look lean, you gotta look cool."*

The truth is that you don't actually have to be a certain age or shape – you just need to look like you are. Entire industries cater to this proposition. This chapter of society doesn't really place much value on being wise, not when you can look young and fresh. This old world of ours has a very curious measuring stick.

This kind of contemporary thinking is in stark contrast to the Bible. The book of Proverbs tells us repeatedly to seek wisdom and avoid foolishness. We are given many examples of what happens when we do, and what happens when we don't. Now there are certain parts of the Bible that are mysterious and obscure, but these truths are very clear, and repeated many times. Some of us might enjoy tracking a mystery, but most of us live our lives on a very practical, street-level basis. We appreciate the practical, accessible and clear principles that we can more easily apply to our daily lives.

Jesus himself used a variety of approaches in His teaching. Some things were very clear and practical, and other things were prophetic or mysterious. *"Why wouldn't He make everything really clear and simple?"* you ask. It's actually quite a simple answer: the Lord expects us to grow. He can speak clearly to little children, and to every person, at every level above that. Jesus could relate to restless teenagers and aged widows, struggling mothers to tense, insecure businessmen, and everything in between. Like a poet, sometimes He wants us to think and ponder what He is talking about.

Through A Child's Eyes

If only we could see through the eyes of a child! When we are young, seeing this way comes easily.

Seeing this way becomes increasingly difficult as we get older. Yet some of the greatest lessons in life come through this way of thinking.

Take a moment to watch kids on a playground. They don't seem to consider outward appearance or skills in playing; in fact, the kids don't even interview each other before choosing. They simply jump right in and start having fun. They don't even try to complicate things. Fun is the whole point.

There is great value in learning as much as we can, but there is also great value in simplicity. Most of us only understand this as we look back. Apparently, we should live life forward but we will understand backwards.

Keep It Simple

My husband – who is not only a great blessing, but such a key part of my story – often says to me: *"Keep it simple."* Confession: That is a good reminder for me because, left unchecked, I tend to complicate things. If I am not aware of this tendency, I can quickly complicate my life to the point of clutter, and not really even notice that just because I am busy doesn't necessarily mean I am accomplishing very much. (This is another reason to have a spouse who is a great match for you.)

In our all consuming day of technology and severe world political crises, everything seems to point to the value of being busy. Oh, they may call it "being connected" or staying "up-to-date", but they really mean being busy all the time. Cellular technology and the Internet are powerful tools, and, properly used, they can help us do all kinds of wonderful things. But in the wrong hands, they can take over your life. You've seen people in a restaurant, sitting in the same booth or table, and all on their cell phones at the same time. In the air, not a word is passing between them, but there is this strange yet fervent electronic conversation happening.

This is not good for any of us. Some of the best conversations I have ever had have been over tables in restaurants. When it is used with thought and intention, technology is quite wonderful. However, if we are slaves to our phones, tablets or computers, then we are simply using the technology in a wrong way. This is something that we can change.

Perhaps things would be different if all the communication had any substance (or worth) – but a large percentage of "messages" are trivial wastes of time. The percentage of important or significant information changing hands is disappointingly small. Communicating something meaningful has great worth – sharing stupid cat videos probably doesn't have any worth.

Desperation and the Fear of Being Left Out

Many seem to be almost desperate to stay "in touch" and "available." There seems to be a strange, almost over-riding fear that we might just miss something. Therefore we simply must read or answer the device immediately! So we waste time every day checking out as many messages as possible. Because we are deathly afraid we will miss something important, we wade into pools of triviality, if not garbage. Some of us waste other peoples' time by sending out mindless drivel. There is no filter. We adhere to no standards. Anything goes. It is the modern version of the Wild West. We may have the quantity part down, but not the quality part.

Don't blame the technology because of these serious problems. Technology is a neutral tool; it is neither good nor bad. The very first printing press was used to print Bibles, the Word of God. Just because later on, some choose to print pornography or hate literature, doesn't mean that the printing press itself is bad. It is just being used poorly, and incorrectly. The press, as a tool, can be used for better purposes again, and illustrate that miracle called Redemption. And, as we shall see, Redemption is the name of the game.

Accountability

Once I realized that, as believers in Jesus we all will give account for **everything** that we do, things began to change in my life and habits. It is a sobering thought to realize that, sometime in the future, I will stand before my Lord and give an account for all that I did in my life.

While none of us can be perfect, we can all certainly increase the standard of our lives by investing our time, energy and creativity into more things that count for eternity, and expend less on celebrated insignificances. I am so grateful for the clear direction on this, given by the Bible.

Proverbs 10:19 is very clear:

> *"In the multitude of words, sin is not lacking; but he who will restrain his lips is wise."*

When You Say Nothing At All

It is more than just about being tasteful, kind of a "less is more" thing. It is about controlling your tongue. There is an old Country song that says: *"You say it best, when you say nothing at all."* Those lyrics may have been written about love between a man and a woman, but this principle of controlling how much you say (as well as the content) applies here. My words count, and they can be powerful. Someday I will have to give an account for them. Many of us will regret some of the things that we said, and few of us will regret things that we considered saying but didn't verbalize.

As a musician and worship leader, I have learned how to pace things musically, and allow for spaces occasionally. Certainly I lead with passion and intensity, but part of what makes music effective is creating some space for the Holy Spirit to have a chance to move. I lead from my heart, and sometimes that is going all out; and other times, it is deliberately holding back, as the Spirit leads me. I don't just do all fast, joyful songs, nor do I do only slow, reflective songs. As one is open to learn from the Teacher, one improves, learns dynamics and makes the worship experience more meaningful and healing. This glorifies God, and is one of the great desires and pleasures of my life.

Game of Deceit

I know a lady who is a master of disguise.
She is so insecure that when she enters a social situation, she quietly adds certain things to her personality, leaves other things out, and even borrows personality traits from others.

Why? Because she is so desperate to be liked, she conducts this personal makeover when she meets new people. The problem with a game of deceit like this is that eventually, this lady will be found out. She has bought into the premise that, if she acts like herself, then nobody will like her, let alone love her. This lady is so fearful of this that she will play her game of deceit in hopes of acceptance and love. How does this behaviour square with Scripture? It doesn't. The Bible tells us clearly:

> *"You shall not take vengeance, nor bear any*
> *grudge against the children of your people;*
> *but you shall love your neighbor as yourself.*
> *I am the LORD"*
> Leviticus 19:18

This can be the most difficult thing for us to do. We may regard this act of loving ourselves as conceit or even arrogance. However it is vital
for us to understand that loving ourselves (in this sense) is actually not a selfish thing to do. It is one of the most selfless things we can do. To be able to love others unconditionally, one needs to be able to love ourselves first. How well we do isn't the most important part.

Loving ourselves is singular, not plural. It is not a comparison, and it is not conceit. The dictionary defines the word "conceit" as:

"An excessively favorable opinion of one's own ability, importance." The key word here is "ability," indicating that we are looking at who we are, not what we can do. A similar word to "conceit" is "arrogance" which is defined as: *"An offensive, overbearing pride."*

This is raising yourself up above others, and feeling pretty good about it.

Gaining the Accurate Perspective

This is an important life lesson that we all need to learn, and to remind ourselves and our families. We are fearfully and wonderfully made!

Like Esther in the Old Testament, we have been called into the Kingdom for such a time as this. We can have great confidence in our God, not in ourselves. We might even feel insignificant or worthless, or ill-prepared for the task ahead. Some of us have obsessed over the wrong choices in our lives for so long that – without God – we are hopeless. We will never be ready.

That is not the end, however. The Bible tells us in the 4th Chapter of Philippians that: *"We can do all things through Christ."* Not in our own strength or by our own cleverness. No, *"all things **through** Christ"!* He is our Partner, He is our Source, He is our ever-present Help in time of need.

Let us remember that the Bible is replete with stories of flawed, passed-over, weak, and very ordinary people. These are the same people whom God called, enabled and used to complete the tasks. Sometimes full-on miracles were involved, and sometimes what God did in and through His people was the miracle.

God has very large, powerful shoulders. He can do great things, and sometimes He does outright impossible things. He wants to work with you. He is not turned off by your past, nor is He intimidated by anything you may ask. He is creative, and He is versatile. He is asking you to partner with Him now. Not when you get your act together and get everything cleaned up.

God wishes that you would begin to understand His love – not only for the world – but especially for you. He wants to heal your brokenness, and He is ready to give you a new start.

You are wanted. You are loved. You are cherished by God. You are chosen!

Chapter 2: **The Man In The Mirror**

"Let Us make Man in Our Image, after Our likeness. And let him (them) have dominion over the fish of the seas and over the fowl of the air, over the cattle and over all the Earth."
Genesis 1:26

"Be fruitful" means to get things done. *"Have dominion"* or *"to subdue"* means to take charge and get it done. The Merriam-Webster Dictionary lists four meanings for the word "subdue":

- To conquer and bring into subjection;
- To bring under control, especially by an exertion of the will; curb < "subdued my foolish fears";
- To bring (land) under cultivation;
- To reduce the intensity of or the degree of; to tone down.

How good are you at any of those?

If we are to subdue the Earth and all that's in it, shouldn't we be able to first subdue ourselves? *"Lord, open our eyes!"* We need a mind shift, a mind that has been transformed.

We are made in the image of God, and while we might sort of understand that to a degree, do we really understand what a wonderful thing it is to be made in God's image? Too often we think we see something, but then later we really see it. Really seeing it is quite different than just seeing it surface. I have had some experience in this regard.

Being Set Up for Failure

All of us have periods in our lives where it just seems a string of things all go wrong. There was a time, not that long ago, where I had one of those "strings" happen to me. To protect the not-so-innocent, I won't go into details here.

The first thing was that an older female (an authority figure) challenged my ability to parent. As a mother, it didn't take long for me to learn that sometimes my decisions weren't popular with my children, and that someone else might have momentarily looked more attractive to them. However, I approached the situation with more prayer and a greater dependency on God, and we weathered that storm.

The second unsettling incident involved a counseling session with a so-called prophet. (I do believe in the office of the prophet, but I have learned that some who claim that, are simply not the real deal.) My husband Jay and I were there for a different reason, but this "prophet" quickly accused me and labelled me a "Jezebel." Hearing this from someone who had the reputation of being a prophet and being able to speak "truth" into peoples' lives, made it difficult to receive.

Having been abused as a young girl, this was particularly hurtful to me. Jay and I were sincerely seeking guidance and direction. All we got were accusations. We didn't stay long, and Jay told me not to take the accusations seriously – but sadly, the damage was already done. I was dazed and confused.

Yes, as a young girl twice I experienced abuse at the hands of trusted male authority figures in my life. Again the exact details are not relevant to this discussion, but both incidents were not only harsh, but life-defining for me. Both times I was innocent and had done nothing to provoke anyone, being a trusting young girl who was victimized by an adult man's lust. And – as has happened too many times in recent years to too many victims – the incidents were not dealt with appropriately. Ultimately, the problems were swept under the proverbial rug, and the perpetrators did not suffer for their actions in violating a young girl. Perhaps their thinking was that if we pretend it didn't happen, then eventually we would believe that it didn't happen. I was the victim – yet the only one who suffered both times, was me.

So, having endured consecutive, unfair and negative encounters with authority figures without any justice, this is the 'string" that led up to this strategic experience of mine, in the shower.

My Aquatic Confessional

I tend to have some of my best times with God in the shower. Often I find that I am more honest with Him there than many other places – my "aquatic confessional." God is a good listener too, as I detail how tough my life is: how some Christian people have been persecuting me, how I don't like it and how I certainly don't deserve it. Once I get some rhythm going, I outline my failures, my weaknesses, my sins, my unanswered prayers, my disappointments, my questions, and much more. I can be almost eloquent in my complaining, wanting God to not only feel sorry for me, but also promise to right all my "wrongs" immediately. I go into great detail how my troubles are not only painful, but undeserved. How uncaring people have victimized me over and over again. (You can almost hear the violins dramatically swelling up in the background, can't you?)

As I finish up on the complaints, I take a quick breath. Not long enough for Him to respond because I am just getting started. (I will discuss with "the still, small" voice a little in greater depth later on.) Back at it, I start to ask God questions:

"God, why am I so misunderstood? Why don't people listen to me? I have been really good for quite a while now, so why are others still hurting me and saying really mean things about me? I am trying, but it doesn't seem to matter. Deep down I am a pretty good person. Why is everybody always picking on me? I am just being real, God. Don't You care? Can't You see me, God? God?"

There isn't any response from anyone. I sigh and go to one of my favorite "go-to" songs when my spirit is down: *"His Eye Is On the Sparrow."* It is a great old song that always brings me comfort. Love those old hymns! This quiets my spirit, like it always does. Time to get back to life. I think to myself: *"Well, at least I can find some measure of comfort in a song."*

The Man in the Mirror

As I exit the shower, I notice that all the mirrors are steamed up. Nothing unusual about that. I wipe a portion of the mirror clean to look at my face ... and I can't believe my eyes! There is another face with incredible eyes in the mirror!

The face is not mine. I turn my head slightly to see the face better. I have never seen eyes like this before. I see eyes that are amazingly loving and compassionate. This is sort of a masculine face, but not really like anyone I've ever seen before.

My first reaction is one of feeling fear – but not a panic form of fear, rather a form of awe and worship. Not knowing whether I should be excited or afraid, I drop to my knees. *"Who is this? Whose eyes are these? Is this Jesus?"* I had just been talking to God, and asking Him for answers. So why am I so surprised when He shows up in my bathroom mirror?

He doesn't actually say anything, but the loving, longing look in those eyes say, well, everything.

Suddenly, emotions overtake me. I begin to laugh. I begin to cry. I feel like I am standing on Holy Ground. I can't control myself. I have to tell somebody. I have to share this with somebody!

Wrapped in a towel, I go to the door and call my 15-year-old daughter to come upstairs. I need to know if she too can see the eyes of the Man in the mirror. I don't have to wait long because as soon as she looks at the steamy mirror, she sees His eyes too. And she begins to cry as well. She has almost exactly the same reaction of mixed feelings that I did. We share this remarkable experience together ... and then I think, *"Who else can I tell?"*

My mother is living across the street, so I call her to come over quickly. By the time my mom arrived, the steam was almost gone, and we could barely see those penetrating, healing eyes. I quickly turn the hot water back on to re-steam the bathroom ... and yes, the wonderful, unsettling eyes are still there. I notice a slightly different expression than what my daughter and I saw, yet His eyes are still amazing and captivating. All three of us stay there, basking in this, not wishing for this special moment to end. We stayed for a long, long time.

His Eye Is On the Sparrow

I thought long and hard about that experience in the shower, and the Man in the mirror. I thought how loving, kind and practical our great God is, to meet me at my point of need. I needed to know that God saw me, and He showed me that He saw me indeed. After this experience I have never, ever doubted that God is really everywhere, all the time. Omnipresent. Or as that old hymn says so well: *"His eye is on the sparrow / And I know He watches me."* I decided to learn more about sparrows.

The Sparrow in the Bible

Several different species of birds in the Bible are called sparrows. They gathered in noisy flocks, and ate grain and insects. Sparrows would often build their untidy nests in the eaves of houses. When they built nests in the Temple, they were not driven away (see Psalms 84:3). The little birds were really social creatures, and a lone sparrow became a symbol of deep loneliness (Psalm 102:7).

The lowly sparrow was also used for offerings in the Temple. Two birds would sell for a copper coin, which was a very low price (less than a quarter in today's currency). Most Temple worshippers brought sacrifices of sheep or goats, so only the very poor and lowly, brought sparrows to the Temple (Leviticus 14:1-7). Sparrows were so insignificant in those days that, if you bought four of them, the seller would likely throw in another one for free (Luke 12:4-7). Actually it was of this "extra" sparrow that Jesus referred to, when He said: *"And not one of them is forgotten before God"* (Luke 12:6). Our Lord was driving this point home: if God is this concerned about the tiny sparrow, how much greater is His love and concern for Mankind, who is immeasurably greater in value than the tiny sparrow!

This is a breathtakingly beautiful picture of the love of God. His Love extends all the way to the tiny sparrow. How much more does He love His children?

Life Lessons Learned From the Sparrow

I made some notes on these life lessons:

1. When I see myself as unworthy or insignificant, God sees me as both significant and important. I was almost frozen in my tracks because of my shame and disillusionment with those who should have – and certainly could have – helped me. Like the Psalmist, my help comes not from man but from

the Lord. Like the Lord demonstrated on the cross, I forgive those who have hurt the little girl that I was.

2. When I am tempted to go back and re-live episodes of misery from my past, I remind myself that I am redeemed by His blood, and completely cleansed and healed. I am able to stand in God's holy presence as his precious, forgiven, restored daughter in whom He delights. God doesn't remember my sins anymore. Ever. I may, and some others may, but the One Who counts, does not. There is great relief and real freedom, in this. I will remember that God has done a great work in me, and has called me to serve Him in His Kingdom.

3. My value to God never changes, regardless of what the stock market does, where the economy goes, or what political system is in power. According to the Word of God, I am fearfully and wonderfully made. My God is the Healer of the broken-hearted; therefore, He sees me as whole.

4. Since I have great value to God, I am called to minister to others in a variety of ways. I sing and lead worship. I create expressions of praise to my Lord in my work, in my home, in my marriage. I show love and compassion to the hurting, and give Godly counsel as often as I have opportunity. I pray for others. I invest in my friends. I give to Godly causes. I am faithful to my God, my husband, my family, my church, my job, and my community to the best of my ability.

Seeing Beyond the Obvious

Once a King decided to honor the greatest subject in his kingdom. When the appointed day arrived, the elaborate event was held in the palace courtyard. Four finalists were brought forward, and everyone expected the King to select the winner, and reward them accordingly.

First, a wealthy philanthropist was presented. In great detail, the King (and all present) was told that because the philanthropist had given huge sums of his wealth to the poor in humanitarian efforts, that this man was very deserving of the honor.

Next, a celebrated physician was asked to step forward, and he was lauded as a brilliant, dedicated doctor who had faithfully served the Kingdom over many years.

Third came a distinguished judge who had a long history of doing justice for the kingdom, because of his great wisdom and the strength of his character.

All three candidates were well-known and impressive.

Finally, an elderly woman was presented. The audience was surprised, as this lady wore humble clothing, and was not really known to the audience. She didn't really look the part of someone being considered for this great honor, particularly in comparison to the other three statesmen.

What had this lady ever accomplished that could compare to the other nominees? She stood there quietly, and there was a look of love in her face, an understanding evident in her eyes. She had a quiet confidence.

The King was somewhat puzzled but also intrigued, and he didn't wish to rush to judgement. He asked who she was. The answer came simply: "Your Majesty, you see the philanthropist, the physician and the judge? This lady was their teacher."

The lady had no fortune, fame or title. Yet what she gave was her life to her students, in order to produce outstanding citizens. There is nothing more Christ-like and powerful than to invest love sacrificially into others. Had he only looked at the outward trappings of success, the King might well have missed seeing who the greatest subject in his kingdom really was.

How important it is for us as individuals to look a little beyond the surface of others? Character is not always obvious. Everyone has value. When we understand that, we can often be Jesus to others.

Remember the Sparrows

"Are not two sparrows sold for a copper coin? And not one of them falls to the ground apart from your Father's will. But the very hairs on your head are numbered; do not fear therefore: you are of more value than many sparrows."
Matthew 10:29-31

I don't pretend that dealing with self-worth issues is easy business. Finding understanding and

Godly counsel is essential, and in some ways it is simple. Simple does not mean necessarily easy. When one is going through inner healing, the process is usually pretty intense. It actually bothered me that the rest of the world seemed to go on its merry way, while I was struggling. Of course, the rest of the world didn't know, so how could they care?

I was a woman who suffered from these issues. I carried this struggle, contradiction of emotions, guilt over unresolved issues until well into my 30s, before I found real freedom and release. Hiding my problems, burying my past, not really coming clean – all contributed to a lot of challenges that took some time to deal with.

I will have much more to share on this in the coming pages, but let me say this clearly: If you can relate to my struggles, if you have been victimized, if you have tried to suppress and hide everything, **please** do not hide any longer! Simply tell God what you feel ... and He will meet you right where you are. He loves you, and longs for your wholeness. Ask Him to guide you to Godly, trustworthy counsellors and people who will love you and help you through whatever is holding you back. Let me tell you, I did. And it has made all the difference – not only in my life, and even my family – I have been released to minister to others, and that is one of the greatest things God calls us to.

Get help for yourself. Then go and help somebody else. Civilla Martin did.

The Story Behind the Great Hymn

In 1904, an American songwriter named Mrs. Civilla Martin went to visit a sick friend in Elmira, New York. Mrs. Martin saw her bedridden friend and asked if she ever got discouraged because of her limitations. The response was immediate:

"Mrs. Martin, how can I be discouraged when my Heavenly Father watches over each little sparrow? I know He loves and cares for me."

Proverbs 15:23 says: *"A man has joy by the answer of his mouth; but a word spoken in due season, how good it is!"* If we are paying attention, we can hear not only some good words, but some life-changing words. Sometimes right in the middle of a lot of useless, wasted words.

I am a Seeker. Finding is reserved only for the seekers. Many times, I have found life-giving words because I was looking for them. Others might miss them. I make an effort not to miss them.

Civilla Martin thought a lot about what her ill friend had said, and she began to write words to a song. You have heard it before:

Why should I feel discouraged
Why should the shadows come
Why should my heart be lonely
And long for Heaven and Home?
When Jesus is my portion
My constant Friend is He

*His eye is on the sparrow
And I know He watches me.*

I am a singer, a musical person. When I am down, *"when I am tempted, whenever clouds arise, when hope seems to die within me, and my songs give place to sighing".... (paraphrased),* that is when I reach out to Him. I need to get closer to my Lord. God's care is immeasurable, and though sometimes it may feel that way, God never leaves us.

*His eye is on the sparrow
And I know He watches me.*

Chapter 3: **Being Heard**

I waited and waited and waited for God. At last He looked; finally He listened.
                                    Psalm 40:1

How to Pay Real Value to Someone

Have you ever felt like you were not being heard? All of us have value, and one of the best ways that we can pay value to others is to take the time and listen to them. Some might think that these are interchangeable terms, but I don't think so. Let me distinguish between hearing and listening.

Most of us hear people, sometimes it's hard not to. How many of us actually listen? We know that we want to be taken seriously ourselves, and to have people pay attention to and absorb what we say, and that will involve listening. Here is how I define these terms:

Hearing is generally more passive and circumstantial, while listening is an active, deliberate act on my part to receive the message(s) that the speaker is sending.

I can hear something that means almost nothing to me, and as the old cliché says: *"It goes in one ear, and out the other."* Not only will I not respond to most of what I hear, I will never remember any of it.

There is good reason that hearing seems to have little value, while we place great value on someone who listens. Much of the communication in our contemporary world actually is of very little value, so it is simply not worth the investment. Yet, at the same time, there are many worthwhile things to consider, and much wisdom available, particularly if we are seeking for it.

Effective listening ties in very well with another spiritual gift: Discernment. Sometimes I probably need that one to operate first – discernment, then listening. One male speaker I remembered hearing, wisely observed: *"Women seem to come with this automatically, most of the time. Men can learn it, but it seems much easier for women."*

A Man Unlike Any Other

It was a warm Fall afternoon in October. He was hard to miss: a larger man with a beard, and salt-and-pepper hair. I was struck by both his physical presence and his very soft, warm voice. Most of the time, we envision big men to have even bigger voices, but this man had both the large stature as well as the soft yet intense voice.

I had just heard him speak in a staff meeting. The subject was leadership, and this wise man spoke about that; and the problems that come from a lack of leadership, and what kind of disappointing results can be expected from poor leadership.

Our staff had just gone through a difficult season with one of our leaders, and we needed some encouragement and direction. Hearing a *bona fide* leader talk about leadership was extraordinary. It would not be exaggerating to say that, in that one hour, my life was changed.

My company gave us an added bonus: each of us was booked for a one-on-one session with the wise man. As I waited for him, I fidgeted nervously. When it was finally my turn, he asked me some questions and then really paid attention to my responses. The wise man took me and my thoughts seriously. He focused his attention completely on our conversation, and was very careful in his comments.

Frankly, I was not used to this. I remember telling him this: "Wow! Somebody has finally heard me!" The wise man wasn't going to marginalize me, or try to fix me in any way. He gave me some sound, practical advice, and then released me with a word of encouragement. What a wonderful experience!

Of course I hadn't pulled the wool over his eyes or anything. He could see that I could be a "needy" person, that I could also be pretty "high maintenance." He saw that I was a seeker. Someone once described me as "a wounded puppy, just looking for some love." Really, it wasn't so much what the wise man said – it was more what the wise man did. God used that wonderful, loving, attentive wise man to help begin a healing process in me, something I really needed. I was ready and willing, and it took a simple act of someone listening to begin the process.

Journey to Significance

There are many great things about God's Word, the Bible. One of my personal favorites is that the text shows the people warts and all. This is not a book of Fairy Tales with perfect, flawless people sparkling through their adventures. No one is candy-coated, or air-brushed.

Take King David, for example. While many regard the Book of Psalms as "all-praise, all-the-time," it's pretty easy to see that much of the book is something quite different. It is true that some of the psalms are spectacular expressions of praise. David didn't write all 150 of the psalms, but he did write more than anyone else. It is apparent that David felt a full range of emotions and moods. (In one early Psalm he asks God to *"break the teeth of my enemies"!*) David's life was both success and failures, and some of his failures were pretty devastating.

In another Psalm, we find David at his low point: full of guilt and shame, and depressed. David could barely believe how low he had gotten. He wasn't sure what to do; his failures had virtually immobilized him. However, wisely David decided to turn to God in his depression. He dealt with his sin by first admitting it, and asking God for His cleansing and forgiveness. David "came clean" – that is, he owned exactly what he had done wrong, and asked God to cleanse him from that.

The Importance of Owning our Sins

Often we are tempted to minimize our sins – let's call them "failures" or "problems." No, let's call them what they are: **SINS!** God calls us to repent of our sins, which means identify them and turn away from them. And live a different, better way.

Getting to that point of owning our sins is challenging for many of us, but it is essential. Own our stuff, and move on. My husband Jay and I have learned over many years that if we own our stuff, confess our issues immediately, then we can move forward. It is when we hide or wait, or try to hold on to the issues, that bind us. The longer we hold them, the worse they hurt us. Our shame binds us. Much like a snowball going down a hill: it picks up speed and momentum as it rolls downward, collecting more snow in the process. It is so dangerous to hold on to things from our past, without resolution or forgiveness. The longer we wait to deal with our sins, the harder and more complicated it can be. A bad past can not only haunt us, but in the end, it can even destroy us.

My Brother From Another Mother

One of God's great blessings to me is a few special friends who love me, believe in me, don't give up on me, and advise me when I choose to listen. One brother (from another mother) is my buddy Dan Hope. (Hope: one of the best last names ever!) Dan is a man of God, a former pastor, and has a great family. His wife Donna is one of my very best friends. Dan is also a very successful salesman. He is the kind of guy who would succeed at whatever he put his mind to.

A sales trainer in his own right, Dan knows the value of repetition when teaching skills. Over the many years I have known him, Dan quotes the end of the verse in Romans 2:4: *"The goodness of God leads us to repentance."* He has quoted that to me many times, in many conversations. Receiving the Word of God requires repetition on our parts, so that we can learn, be challenged, be reminded, be instructed, and be encouraged. (*"Thank you, Dan Hope, for making sure I remember this truth!"*)

Pithy Summary

So, everyone: let's keep short accounts. When we sin, let's all agree to deal with it immediately. There is absolutely no value in hanging on to shame. Remember: it is the goodness of God that leads us to repentance. As soon as we repent, God forgives and no longer holds that against us. It is so simple. We are the ones who complicate it. Jesus did a complete and thorough work on the cross.

It is finished! Now, let's walk it out.

Chapter 4: **Lies, Suppression and Control**

I believe in order. I believe in freedom. For some, these concepts are mutually exclusive. Not for me. Not from what I read in the Bible. Not from what I know of the character of God.

These days everybody is an expert. People don't just have ordinary opinions or ordinary points of view anymore. They have expert opinions.

Recently walking through a large *Chapters* Bookstore, I was almost overwhelmed with the wide variety of books on every possible subject that you might be interested in, and many subjects that you are not. There are certainly more books out there than one could ever read in a lifetime, and of course, more titles on more subjects are being added all the time.

Particularly interesting to me are commonly called "self-help" books, so I wandered over to that section. It was huge! Row after row of books telling the reader how to do (what seemed like) pretty much anything. I read many of the titles, and was impressed with how much information is out there just in this "self-help" category.

I pulled out three interesting titles, and flipped through the pages, paying attention to the sentences written in a **bold font.** It seemed like all the authors spoke in absolute terms (*"this is the right way to do this"*) and with an impressive amount of authority (*"believe me, I know what I am talking about; here are my credentials and experience ..."*). Yet I laughed because opinions on the same subject varied wildly between the books. Each of the three titles claimed to be completely correct and absolutely the best information on that subject. How does that work?

This is one reason I suggest to you, while you are reading *this* book: please know that **your most important Teacher is the Holy Spirit.** Yes, this book is my story and things are communicated from my life, experience and philosophy, but if something you read does not resonate with you in your heart, or if you hear/feel/sense that it is contrary to the Word of God but is simply my opinion, please disregard it. I have bathed this project and message in prayer, and my intent is to honor Jesus Christ in all I write, but I am still a human being.

I am a sincere woman of God who takes this responsibility of teaching and sharing seriously. I have a team of friends who are supporting me in this effort. What a blessing! They are praying that the message which Jesus wants each reader to read comes through, above everything else. Several friends in particular have been "bathing me in prayer" during all the stages of preparation and writing.

You and I can trust the Holy Spirit in this. In the Gospels, He describes Himself as *"the Way, the Truth, and the Life"* (John 14:6), and that is stated so that we can have full confidence in His Word.

Back to Freedom

You must have heard this many times: *"Children are to be seen and not heard."* I was taught this. This was widely taught in many circles. And it is a lie.

Children – as well as adults – need the freedom to express themselves without being told to shut up and sit down. Can you guess what I might have heard growing up? God actually created us to be expressive, creative, intuitive. How can we learn to walk in these things if we are routinely suppressed and shut down? How can that negative response not affect us? If we are not given the opportunity to grow in these vital parts of our personalities, what are the consequences?

It is a given that we cannot have chaos, that a reasonable amount of order is needed. That is not what I am talking about here. In my studies, I have found that most children who grow up in a restrictive environment tend to become chameleons: easy adapters, kaleidoscopes. Those children will find a way to fit into the environment in which they are placed. Here is a fascinating case study:

A team of curious scientists gathered a significant number of fleas, which they put into glass jars. Once the fleas were inside, clear lids on the jars were screwed on. Immediately, all the fleas made it their mission to jump out of the jars. For about 15 minutes, the fleas jumped and bounced back off the inside of the lids.

Eventually, somehow a consensus developed among the fleas that the lid wasn't coming off. They continued jumping, but not as high as before. Presumably to avoid those head crashes. All the fleas jumped about an inch short of the lid. None of them ventured any higher. That continued for another 15 minutes.

Then the scientists quietly removed the lids, to see if the fleas would now jump out of the jars.

They didn't jump out. All the fleas were now adjusted to the new reality that the jars were inescapable. They continued jumping, but never beyond that inch from the top. The fact is that the fleas could have now jumped out of the jar at any time, but they had quickly become accustomed to (what they thought to be) their new reality. They adapted to confinement.

People are not fleas, but this is still a very valid lesson for us. What goal(s) have we given up on too quickly because things didn't quite work out the way we expected initially? We must remain vigilant because sometimes a small change – such as a lid being removed – can make all the difference in the world.

The Bird Cage

Often I am asked to pray for others. And I love doing it, as I regard praying for others a real privilege. Once, after a friend shared a long, heartfelt conversation that related to her very difficult life in detail, she asked me to pray that she would find freedom. As I began to pray, I saw a vision. (Remember: this kind of prayer is a collaborative exercise with our Savior.) I shared this lovely vision with her:

She was a bird in a beautiful cage, an ornate one with a wrought-iron door. The door was wide open. She, the bird, was inside but she would not fly free. She seemed frozen by her insignificance. True, her environment had changed by the door being open, freedom beckoned – but she couldn't see anything beyond her own ways (her old habits, her old ways of thinking) so she couldn't see that the cage door was open.

I hope this is clear. I am speaking to many right now: the cage door is open, so fly out! Get free!

Remember these truths:

- The pains of the past do not control the pleasures of tomorrow, unless you allow them.
- When the winds around us are blowing too strongly to head in one direction, change the direction of your sail.
- Change is inevitable, but growth is optional. Do not fear change. Welcome growth.
- Walk into your significance. Don't postpone things until you understand everything perfectly. This is your season!

Guard Your Mind

Our minds are very powerful things. Yet our minds are sometimes too easily influenced by others' opinions. Be aware that the Bible says we will become like those with whom we surround ourselves. Not that we are easily programmed or manipulated, but that we must be careful so that we are not around people who are not going where we want to go, where we feel called to go.

I am not suggesting that we only surround ourselves with those whom we believe will further us, because that would be selfishness. We must choose carefully whom we allow to speak into our lives. Choose those who love you, who will be honest with you, and who will care enough to confront you when you are making unhealthy choices.

Since none of us like to be judged (have you ever met anyone who does?), let us also be careful not to judge others. Please don't expect perfection, but watch for steady growth. Love and accept your "group" for who they are at that time, and where they are at. Jesus accepts us, and works with us where we are.

You can know the Holy Spirit intimately. But don't attempt to be the Holy Spirit. Be you. And please remember Whose you are.

In counseling, I often find that one of the real problems people have is that they simply do not know who they are in Christ. **Identity is not in what you do, it is in who you are.**

I know that sometimes it may feel we are abandoned and all alone, but the truth is that help and direction from God is always available, if we are seeking Him for it. We all have to learn to deal with and control our feelings. Our feelings should never control us. Sadly, many of our peers do let their feelings control them, and the negative fruit is very evident. Yet, as a daughter or son of God, we can do much better.

Life-Changing Truth: You Are Significant

A lot of you are dealing with issues of self worth. You don't feel very good about yourselves simply because of the things you have been through, possibly the things you have done or that have been done to you. I can relate to this.

God draws all men unto himself, I am so thankful for that. He draws us back when we go astray. I remember after Roman (my adopted dad) passed away, I wasn't dealing with it very well. As a matter of fact, I wasn't dealing with it at all. I would say that I had derailed.

My mother, with concern for her daughter. knew how much I loved Darlene Zschech. She was a huge influence in my life mostly in the area of worship. She happened to be teaching at a conference in British Columbia, our neighboring province, and Mom asked if I wanted to go. I said yes only because I didn't want to miss the opportunity of meeting Darlene.

This conference would be the life-changing shift of significance for Kelly.

One of the speakers got up on stage and asked the question "what if I gave you this fifty dollar bill, would you take it"? I bet you would. Of course everyone there could see the value of the dollar bill. She proceeded to crumple the bill up into a ball and then asked if it changed the value of the bill? She then threw it on the floor, took her foot and rubbed it into the carpet, (this is what hit me... Bam) again asking if it still held it's value. "Well, she said, "What if I do this?" she sunk it into a glass of water, while she was getting it wet, she talked about a savior that sees us as the highest valued thing on this earth, so much so that He gave up his own life so that mine could be saved. She asked again, "does it still hold it's value, does it lessen the value?" Lastly she ripped it in half and raised the same question one last time, "does the value of this fifty dollar bill still hold the same value?" The whole audience with a loud breath gasped Yes. This was my ah ha moment.

My friends, you have all learned a valuable lesson while reading this. No matter what was done to the fifty dollar bill, we all would have taken it because we understand that it didn't decrease in value. It was still worth fifty dollars.

This woke me up immediately. I couldn't believe how much this illustration impacted me. I have never been the same. Understanding the meaning that very moment that I truly was significant and valued. That nothing someone does to me or what I do to myself can lessen my value or significance. Even if I was stepped on or ripped in half, I was still Kelly and my value remains the same. What happens to me may bruise me or even break me but it will never change the value of who I am.

We are significant. We don't have to find our significance or attempt to earn our significance. No, we already have been given that. What a powerful statement! Let me say it again:

We are significant!

Now, it is very possible we may not know this truth. It is also possible we may not choose to walk in this truth. But this is the truth, and what does the Bible say? *"You shall know the truth, and the truth shall set you free!"* (John 8:32). The desire of my heart is that you are aware of this, and have a personal awareness of who you are in Christ.

Let me talk directly to the sisters for a moment. It is very clear to me that most of we sisters spend far too much time striving to ***"be":***

- to **be** seen
- to **be** heard
- to **be** valued
- to **be** romanced.

All of these (very legitimate) desires are natural desires of a woman. What a change can take place when we realize that all of these can be achieved.

Biblical Beauty

> *"Your beauty should not come from outward adornment, such as braided hair, the wearing of gold jewelry and fine clothes. Instead, it (your beauty) should be that of your inner self, the unfading beauty of a gentle and quiet spirit.*
>
> 1 Peter 3:3-4

Another translation renders verse 4 this way:

> *"But let it be the hidden person of the heart, with the incorruptible ornament of a gentle and quiet spirit, which is very precious in the sight of God."*

Not pointing any fingers here, I have worked for many years in a profession (Flight Attendant) where beauty and physical appearance are a major component to the industry. Many young people, men and women spend hours and money on improving their appearance, including Botox injections and liposuction. They will tell you it is a preventative measure. Preventing what? The natural process of aging? As far as the outward appearance goes, I make no apology that I enjoy making the most of what I have, of looking good. The last time I checked with my husband, Jay was on board as well. That is part of living contented, for me. However, I also know that looking good is not the most important thing, according to the Bible.

In Greek, the word *"clothe"* means "put on this garment." Sometimes we will "put on" someone else's personality or character. I call this "borrowing someone else's anointing." This is not something we need to do.

When God created us, He made it clear that He knew what He was doing. God, the original Creator, created a unique and special individual, not a copy of someone else. How many years did I spend trying to change myself and be someone else? Why do we think in such terms?

Allow me to clarify. I absolutely believe in personal growth and challenging ourselves to ever greater wisdom. The directive (command) here is simply building on the foundation that is already there. This passage says it very clearly: it is all about the heart, not the outward appearance. It is what's inside that counts.

No Expectations?

We need to accept one another. We should not marginalize or judge one another. We need to have expectations for ourselves to live up to, but not for others. That expectation is God's favor in our lives. Hear my heart, Sisters: in my marriage, I used to think that if I had no expectations, then I could not be disappointed. That wasn't Godly thinking, however, because I was simply shutting my mouth and lowering my standards. It was a form of false humility. In actuality, humility is total dependence on God. It is not weak, silent, quiet, or meek.

We live in a generation, a society, that demands instant results. The faster the better. There is a place for speed, but our society has little patience and allows very little room for process. God needs us to wait on Him, and get the results in His time. His timing is precise and perfect. How different are God's ways from many of ours!

Just Be You: It Is Your Greatest Anointing

Learn how to love yourself in the here and now. We are not talking about "down the road" – it is about now. God is ready to use you now, where you are, in your work, in your sphere of influence. I hope this is sinking in: your journey is part of your purpose. You might be called to save a nation, like Esther (see Esther 4:14).

If I sound urgent about this, it is because I have been there myself. For years, my identity was in what I could do, not in who I was. If I wasn't leading worship or at least singing on the team, I felt useless. Many components of my life were similar to that. If I didn't receive praise for, say, cleaning my home, I didn't enjoy doing it. I was stuck on performance. My sense of personal value was tied into being appreciated for what I did.

I clung tightly to the reins of my life, and didn't let the Lord lead me. It took me several years of brokenness to realize that my personal value had nothing to do with my performance. The issue was not what I did – the issue was Whose I was. When I decided to let go, God took over. That is when good things started to happen.

Psalm 32:9 discusses being controlled by a bit and bridle, like a horse. Positionally, God is ultimately in control anyway, but He is a Gentleman and doesn't force us. He gives us this choice:

"You can do this the easy way, or you can do this the hard way. It is up to you."

It is amazing that God wants to collaborate with us in this way!

He who falls on this stone will be broken to pieces, but he on whom it falls will be crushed.
Matthew 21:24

Better to fall upon the Rock than to have the Rock fall upon you!

Good Friends, Real Friends, Are One of God's Greatest Blessings

A good friend – one who loves you – tells you the truth. Right when I needed to hear it, one good friend sat me down and carefully told me that I spent far too much time trying to be what others wanted me to be, when I would be much better off just being me. This took courage for my friend, but it was a real breakthrough moment for me. I could just be me ... and that was exactly the best thing I could hear! This became the best thing I could do. I took stock of who I was in Christ and what He has already equipped me to do. Knowing this was so liberating! It took all kinds of pressure off my shoulders. I am a significant woman. I am **free to be!**

Wise Counsel

You may have heard the name of a well-known and highly-respected Christian leader, Loren Cunningham. Among many other achievements in the Kingdom of God, Loren founded the very effective, world-changing ministry of *Youth With A Mission* (YWAM). A good friend of mine met and worked with YWAM teams in nine countries of Asia, and he has nothing but admiration and respect for the commitment YWAM-ers display. YWAM is an awesome, God-honoring ministry that has been very effective all over the Globe, and has also stood the test of time.

Loren is a great writer, and I would like to quote from one of his articles:

"Your greatest satisfaction will come to you as you submit to God and fulfill the purpose you were created for. God has gifted you to do what He has called you to do. He would never ask you to do something without giving you the ability to accomplish it, nor would He give you a gift and then tell you never to use it. The calling God has given you is an awesome responsibility. We have learned, through more than forty years of leading hundreds of thousands of missionary volunteers, that if you try to do what someone else has been gifted and called to do, you will end up frustrated. If you get out of the area of your calling, you will end up confused."

What wise, practical counsel! I love knowing who I am, and Whose I am. God can open doors that no Man can.

I recall a prayer time about 2:30 a.m., walking the floor in my living room. Yes, I was asking for His wisdom and direction, but at the same time, I was questioning His plans. He had called me to a very specific task, and I complained that I didn't have enough knowledge and that, frankly, I wasn't really worthy for the task. As clear as a bell in my spirit, God reminded me of a scripture:

The One Who calls you is faithful, and He will do it.
1 Thessalonians 4:24

That was perfect, and cleared things up immediately! I moved out in faith, and God used me for His glory.

A Big God

It is an interesting mix that God looks for: we must move out in faith, yet our dependence is completely on Him. He is a good God, and He is a big God. We must never try to get past the point of trusting Him and believing that he knows precisely what He is doing. God made you ... so just be you. Be the very best you that you can be. Be free to be!

Chapter 5: **Actions Do Speak Louder Than Words**

"Can I tell you something, Kelly? You are a very sweet person. I like you a lot. But Kelly, you are trying way too hard. I know you want to be liked. We all do. But Kelly, you have taken this to a whole new level. You are not being true to yourself. The Kelly I know is a great person, but what you are showing me is somebody who looks a lot like my friend Kelly but isn't really acting like her. You are almost acting like someone else! You would be so much more relaxed and happier if you would just be yourself!"

This speech came from a woman who is my friend. It was blunt. It was direct. My friend wasn't trying to be diplomatic, because she felt it was essential to get my attention. Most of us prefer to be addressed gently, with a lot of love. There are times, however, when we need to be direct and even passionate, in order to make the point.
Bam! Bam! Bam!

Of course, this all came too fast for me to process in detail. At first, I was stumped. *"What did she mean by that? Of course I was being myself – who else would I be? How dare she speak to me that way!"* Suddenly a scripture came to my mind:

"Open rebuke is better than love carefully concealed" Bam! Then the very next verse: *"Faithful are the wounds of a friend, but the*

kisses of an enemy are deceitful." Bam! This is Proverbs 27:6. Same chapter, verse 17:

"As iron sharpens iron, so a man sharpens the countenance of his friend." Bam!

The truth does have a sobering effect on us, if we let it. Was I ever blind! I had become so good at adapting to those around me, or to the culture I was in, that I actually had forgotten who Kelly was! I am glad to say my friend still hung in there with me, though it was actually years later that I finally understood what she meant by her statement, and these two questions:

Question One: Have you become what you think others want you to be?

Question Two: Do you even know who you are?

The Not-So-Great Pretender

Even when I was dating, I would sometimes pretend that I enjoyed a certain genre of music, when really I didn't. I also said I enjoyed cooking, when I didn't know how to boil water. Or going to certain movies that I really didn't like although others did. Why? Because I had decided the most important thing was to be liked. So I adjusted myself to appear to be something I really was not.

If I came upon a conversation in which I wanted to participate, I would even make up stories so I could fit into the discussion. There is a name for this: it is called **lying**. People, like me, who were willing to lie in order to fit in, are called **liars.**

Lying is an insidious habit. We generally have two reasons to lie: (1) to protect ourselves; (2) to fit in. I excelled at both. Like most liars, I simply didn't consider the long-term results of lying. Guess what? Our lies will find us out. The old joke states that *"he is only lying when his lips are moving."* I suspect we can do even worse: we can lie in our thoughts and deeds, not just with our words.

When we begin to understand that significance makes us valuable and there is never a need to lie, things can change for the better, and quickly.

Lying is a serious sin. *"Really? How serious can lying be?"* In the last book of the Bible, in Revelation Chapter 21, there is a very specific, easy-to-understand verse describing certain kinds of sinners. Here is the list:

*But the cowardly, unbelieving, abominable, murderers, sexually immoral, sorcerers, idolaters, and **all liars** will have their part in the lake which burns with fire and brimstone.*
                                                            Revelation 20:7-10

God always advocates for the Truth. The Truth is always worth striving for. God actually hates lying. So should we.

Variations on the Theme

Another way that we lie (to ourselves) and deceive (others) is to put others down in order to raise ourselves up. Somehow we must believe that we will feel more valuable and better about ourselves if we lower others. Why else would we need to talk about others in a negative way?

Here is the truth: only when we can love ourselves can we then love others. *"How do we love ourselves?"* Thank you for asking! We love ourselves by (1) accepting who we are; and (2) work towards bettering ourselves, finding whom we want to be. Remember, a mirror cannot lie. When we look into a mirror, we see all things. How do you see yourself?

Can I Change?

Say to yourself: *"I have the power to change me! With God's help and forgiveness, the process can begin."* God is our Father, and He knows exactly what we need. A good parent loves their child, no matter what the consequences. When we remind ourselves of Whose we are, this takes the focus off of us. God is our Strength, our Source, our ever-present Help in times of trouble.

Nancy Sims wrote the following – **"Ten Don'ts To Remember, A Creed to live by:**

1. Don't undermine your worth by comparing yourself to others. It is because we are different that each of us is special.
2. Don't set your goals by what other people deem important. Only God really knows what is best for you.

3. Don't take for granted the things that are closest to your heart. Cling to them as you would your life – for without them, life is meaningless.

4. Don't let life slip through your fingers by living in the past or by living in the future. Live in the **now.** By living your life one day at a time, you live all the days of your life.

5. Don't give up when you have something to give. Nothing is really over until the moment you stop trying.

6. Don't be afraid to admit that you are less than perfect. It is this fragile thread that binds us to each other.

7. Don't be afraid to encounter risks. It is by taking risks and chances that we learn to be brave.

8. Don't shut love out of your life by saying it is impossible to find. The quickest way to receive love is to give love. The fastest way to lose love is to hold it too tightly. And the best way to keep love is to give it wings.

9. Don't dismiss your dreams. To be without dreams is to be without hope. To be without hope is to be without purpose.

10. Don't run through life so fast that you forget not only where you have been but also where you are going. Life is not a race but a disciplined journey to be savored each step of the way.

"Feelings, Nothing More Than Feelings"

Years ago, Morris Albert struck a chord with an international hit song called *"Feelings."* It was a secular song and it appealed to many people. It resonated with millions around the world because we all have to deal with feelings.

Feelings can be very powerful. Some become victims to their feelings. Some are motivated by their feelings. Some are crippled by their feelings. Like many other spiritual truths, feelings can be positive or negative, beneficial or a virtual waste of time. It all depends on our attitude toward our feelings. Since all of us have to deal with our feelings, the same question arises: *"Do I control my feelings or do my feelings control me?"*

"Who made my feelings?" Well, ultimately God made our feelings, though He gives us permission to use them any way we wish. Like our tongues, our feelings can do much good or much damage. It depends on whether you control your feelings or your feelings control you.

It is part of God's plan that we master our feelings. Properly managed, our feelings can bring out many great things in us. Sadly, this is the exception, not the rule. Everywhere we turn, it seems there are people who are completely mastered by their feelings, and most of those are negative feelings of fear ... doubt ... greed ...lust ... hate... and so many others. The Church should be the exception to this reality. The Body of Christ should be a safe, welcoming, forgiving, supportive place of refuge for hurting, wounded people. Let us be people whose feelings bring out the best in ourselves and in others. Let kindness and compassion be very apparent, particularly to those who are hurting.

Broken People

Undeniably, God chooses to use broken people. If we have not been broken yet, it is certain that we will be at some point in our lives. Brokenness is a weak state ... and yet here is something incredible! When we are weak, then He is made strong.

God has always allowed Man's weakness to validate Man's immeasurable need of God's rescue and God's adequacy. If we allow Him to do so, He can and will work in us, and He will use us. We are not the Message, but only the conduit used to deliver His Message. This is God's amazing system: He uses human beings as His hands and feet – and the world cannot only be reached but changed!

You would think that God would select the talented, the attractive and the winsome. No, God's choice has always been the ordinary, and usually He picks the under-dogs! The world identifies people as *"the woman most likely to succeed"* – God waltzes right past them and finds *"the least likely to succeed."* Check it out.

A Bunch of Losers

As we read through the Bible, we see that the great men and women whom God selected started out broken, but He used them anyway:

- **Noah** got drunk
- **Abraham** was too old
- **Isaac** was a daydreamer

- **Jacob** was a liar
- **Leah** was too ugly
- **Joseph** was abused
- **Moses** had a stuttering problem
- **Gideon** was afraid
- **Samson** was a womanizer
- **Rahab** was a prostitute
- **Jeremiah** and **Timothy** were too young
- **David** had an affair, and was a murderer
- **Elijah** was suicidal
- **Isaiah** preached naked
- **Jonah** ran from God
- **Naomi** was a widow
- **Job** went bankrupt
- **John** the Baptist ate bugs
- **Peter** denied Christ
- **Martha** worried about everything
- One disciple fell asleep while praying
- The **Samaritan woman** was divorced and remarried many times over
- **Zacchaeus** was too small
- **Paul** was too religious
- **Lazarus** was dead.

Take a good look at that list. It is a bunch of broken people! That is how many of the great heroes of the Bible started out. In some cases, it wasn't their fault ... in some cases, it was. The point is that God can take anybody who is willing, and use them – if they cooperate with Him. I suspect that many of us can be encouraged because while we may have some problems, most are not nearly as serious as some of our listed people. God is interested in us. He is interested in using us.

Chapter 6: **Own It and Move On**

As children, most of us had parents who tried to do their best in raising us. Most of us were trained to tell the truth, and we learned that it was wrong to lie. One would think that honesty and integrity are basics that every child learns. There were some pretty negative consequences for telling lies, deceiving others and even exaggeration. **Tell the truth:** this is a core value of the Bible from beginning to end. Sadly, our society has deteriorated in many ways where now ethics are often situational, and truth is no longer something solid but it is fluid and open to interpretation.

How Did We Get Here?

The world that we live in today appears to be riddled with deception. Around every corner there seems to be another lie. The issue that I have with this is that (once again) society has found a way to excuse the lie, and candy-coat it. What ever happened to the truth, to honesty? Does that still exist?

Once upon a time, deception was quite rare. Now, sad to say, it seems deception has almost become the norm. Some of us believe our own lies. How did we get to this?

Our minds are an incredible and powerful tool that will either work for us, or will work against us. For many, learning to lie happens at a very young age. The "principle of momentum" fits here. Once we get used to lying, we justify our behavior and label lying as something else, using terms like "enhancement." It is apparently easy to do ... and even easier with practice.

The Key to Success

Learn to recognize the lie while it is still small. If we catch it as soon as it tries to enter our minds, we can shut it down quickly. My mom used this advice: "Nip it in the bud" – meaning to stop the lie from growing.

Picture a tree ... and your thought is the trunk of the tree. If we add to the thought (the lie), then branches begin to grow and the tree gets bigger. If we water that thought, the growth accelerates. I have found that when I entertain a lie, encourage it a little, the story grows until I can actually believe it.

When I was about nine years old, I created a story in my mind that I stewed on for about ten minutes. This story became a reality to me. Though I had made it up and there was nothing true about it, somehow I deceived myself into believing this story. Later, I was confronted about this tall tale, and I defended it because I had talked myself into believing it. Suddenly it hit me that my whole story was not true. I had to own it. I had to go back and apologize.

Responsibility vs. Owning It

Often we hear this term: *"Take responsibility for your actions."* Taking responsibility is good, but owning (admitting, confessing) it is better. Let's define some of these terms.

- **Responsibility**: the state or fact of being accountable or to blame for something.
- **Accountable**: required to be responsible for something.
- **Own**: to admit that something is true.

Of the three terms, owning it, is usually the most difficult to do. There is a sequence: we must **own** it first in order to take **responsibility** and then become **accountable.** If I don't own it, someone else has to. If not me, then who? Which brings us to the Blame Game.

The Blame Game

Another definition is called for, and the word is "**blame**": to say or think that a person or thing is responsible for something bad that has happened. One sees the Blame Game being played frequently. Two environments quickly come to mind: (1) the legal courtroom; and (2) the political arena. There are many others. One very common strategy for addressing conflict is to ascribe blame. There are many scenarios possible; here are three:

1. An authority figure who fails to maintain appropriate ethical standards;
2. A family member guilty of abusing a child or a spouse;

3. A corporation with an agenda by setting up a "fall guy," someone who will fail and make dismissal easier.

Any of these (and there are many more) are not easy to own, but that is precisely why it is essential that we do own them! What would the business world be like if people owned their wrong-doing instead of pointing the finger at someone else? By owning our stuff, we exhibit honesty and humility – two character traits rarely found in the business arena today.

The Process Can Be Challenging

Owning it will be a time of inward searching, quiet thinking and honest reflection. One of the most difficult things we have to do involves taking a long, hard look at what we do and what we have done. Discovering the reasons and motivations can be disturbing. Funny, it is never easy to admit our own wrongdoings. If discovered, we hope for mercy, gentleness and understanding from our team. Yet we can be quite hard on our co-workers who don't see or admit their wrong-doings. There is a word for this: **hypocrisy**. Hypocrisy comes from a Greek word for "actor" – one who wears a mask and pretends to be someone other than who he is. In the theatre, acting can be a wonderful thing – in real life, acting is never a wonderful thing. We never want to be the "great pretender."

On the surface, blaming others seems so much easier than admitting what we did ourselves. None of us like pressure, and often blaming someone else seems to take the pressure off us and place it elsewhere. This is why so many people do it so much of the time. I must admit that I am not a fan of looking back to past issues, particularly involving shame and blame. It is not merely uncomfortable – it can be painful. Pain is never fun. However, doing this is necessary if we need to know whether this issue is a problem in our lives or not.

It is not only major life issues that need to be dealt with – smaller things can be problematic as well. This is easily seen in relationships. She forgot to pack enough diapers ... or he didn't clean up the dog poop in the back yard before the snow fell. Sound familiar? *"You didn't _____"* (fill in the blank). Too often, this is the first thing off the end of our tongues. Shouldn't it be: *"You are right! I should have done _____."*

Even in conversation, we need to be careful not to manipulate with blame. For some, it might be a survival mechanism; other times, it is defensive gossip: *"Since I can't cope with my own stuff, I will deflect the conversation and talk about someone else's flaws. Anyone but me!"* This behavior starts at a very young age, and gets easier as we get older. The key is to catch it early in life and deal with it promptly.

Tell Yourself the Truth

Sometimes things that happen can be so painful that we try to tell ourselves something else, just to cope or survive. There is nothing wrong with trying to protect yourself but we must always do that within the context of truth. Kids say, *"He did it"* or

"She made me do it" or *"I can't help it."* Deflection may seem to work short term, but it doesn't in the long term.

Yes, I understand that sometimes we are not completely to blame, but we never need to let something negative or hurtful define who we are.

I could hide behind that too. As a 13-year-old girl, I was sexually abused not once but twice, and by two different men. As you can imagine, this was a very difficult issue to deal with as an adult. Even though none of the incidents were my fault, I still had to deal with them. I didn't understand that, and the adults around me were not much help either.

Since I didn't understand, I ended up allowing these very unfortunate incidents to define me ... and I gave myself permission to live as less than my potential. In other words, I held myself back because I didn't know how to deal with my stuff! I did not have to own the abuse, but I was not truthful to myself, and used that to justify some very unwise choices later in life. Mentally, I blamed the abuse for my own poor actions. *This* is what I had to own: I had to own my subsequent actions.

How about some really good news? As an adult, every day in my life I have the power of choice. Why? Because His mercies are new every morning. New beginnings! God is faithful to keep His promises, whether or not we deserve them (we don't), because He is a God of His Word. Here is a great verse about God telling the truth and what results from Him doing that:

> *"God is not a man that He should lie. Nor a son of man that He should repent. Has He*

said, and will He not do it? Or has He spoken, and will He not make it good?"
                                    Numbers 23:19

Those evil twins, Shame and Blame, are known to freeze many of us in our tracks. Looking back in order to properly deal with old issues is necessary. The silver lining is this: "Looking back at our past can also serve to remind us that today is a gift!" Staying there, constantly rehearsing our past faults, wrong choices and unfortunate mishaps will keep us frozen in shame. If we can keep our eyes on our Heavenly Prize, then we really can move on. Hallelujah!

As I consider this important issue, I realize that surprisingly few people are really very concerned with these issues. To meet an honest person, a woman of true Biblical integrity, is quite rare. I wish that encountering people of integrity was a much more frequent occurrence in my life. What can I do about that? Well, it's a small start, but I can make the effort to be a person of integrity myself, and live my life that way every day. That is what God asks of me, and I am willing to do that for Him. Let's own it, and move on.

Chapter 7: Mindset, Unity and a Music Festival

"As a man thinks in his heart, so is he."
Proverbs 23:7

Max Yasgur's Farm

I would now like to take you back in time a few years. The year is 1969, the season is summer, and we are out in the country on the East Coast of the United States. From every direction, you can see vehicles converging on a farm in upstate New York – a farm that belongs to Max Yasgur. When you get close to Yasgur's farm, you notice the diversity of those pilgrims: some old, many younger, some fat, many skinny, some sad, many happy, and all curious. Every religion, every financial strata, every kind of seeker imaginable. Everyone seems to have expectancy written all over their faces. Filled with anticipation and willingness to do whatever was required, yet not really knowing what would be required of them.

The event sponsors said that the arrivals had begun from the early afternoon of the day before; and even after the area filled up, people just kept coming. Wondering what would happen, and completely ready to jump right in. Then something unexpected began happening: people who had never met before were greeting each other and wrapping their arms around each other as if they were reunited with old friends. All night, the crowds kept coming relentlessly, and into the next morning, bringing the estimated numbers to 500,000. Half-a-million strong. Everyone was looking at a large wooden stage surrounded by sound system towers aimed back at the audience.

When the massive concert began, the crowd responded in unity, and listened to dozens of performers offering a wide variety of musical styles. The audience response was unlike any of the performers had ever witnessed. This event was scheduled for three days, with the first day's offering being mostly folk, blues and acoustic music, with the heavier rock-and-roll music scheduled for Days 2 and 3. The performers played through the day, through the evening and on through the night.

The only thing that stopped the show was a couple of summer showers that drenched everyone. As soon as things dried out a little, much of the audience began playing together in the mud. The music whipped back up, with many of the leading artists of the day. Everyone knew that something very special was happening.

It was called "Woodstock" – one of the true watershed events of the 20th century.

People, People, and More People

One description of Woodstock went like this: *"Gathered that weekend in August 1969 were liars and lovers, prophets and profiteers. They made love, they made money, and they made a little history. Arnold Skolnick, the artist who designed the famous Woodstock dove-and-guitar logo, described it this way: 'Something was tapped, a nerve, in this country. And everybody just came ....'"*

Monumental as the festival was, it wasn't quite as ideal as legend has since painted it. However there were surprisingly few problems (deaths, injuries, overdoses, etc.), considering the massive numbers and incredible lack of facilities. Much has been made of the (mostly) peaceful way that almost everyone behaved over that three-day period. Peaceful, yet hedonistic. For our discussion, let us focus on that incredible sense of unity.

Really, it wasn't just about the music, the drugs, the drinking, or even the location. What it was about was the people and their way of thinking. For all the diversity, there was a pervasive unity that prevailed for the three or so days. Yes, music was the initial catalyst, but what made Woodstock significant was far deeper.

My husband Jay and I have often commented that we were born a few years too late. In one sense, we would have loved to have been a part of the Woodstock Generation.

What Made Woodstock So Special?

There were three or four similar festivals in several parts of the U.S. that summer, all within days of Woodstock. Most featured many of the same artists as Woodstock. The other events may have had some levels of success, but none of them are even remembered now. Why then did Woodstock stand apart?

1. It was the unity. All kinds of people – male and female, many different ages, from many different strata of life – all converged together ... and though they were extremely crowded, amazingly everyone got along. There was a prevailing desire to love and accept everyone, and not have any expectations of anyone else to change. When resources ran short, everyone shared. Of all the festivals that summer, Woodstock also had the largest crowd. By far. Help came in from unexpected sources too: dozens of doctors, police and military personnel volunteered their time and resources, providing helicopter transportation and on-site medical facilities, all for free. This was unusual because at that time in history, members of the military and law enforcement were often held in contempt by most younger people. The *"Thank you for your service"* concept – which is quite common today – was still decades away.

2. The event was filmed. We don't have to rely on people's memories or even written records. We can watch it on film and have a very similar experience even today. Of course, the Woodstock film was edited, but the film still captured not only the Event but the Unity. Another 1969 festival (the Seattle Pop Festival) was musically just as good (or better) than Woodstock, but no one had a camera rolling, so the evidence is not nearly as compelling.

3. The movie *"Woodstock"* was what put the promoters in the black. On the first day, peace-loving hippies overran the temporary fences and made the festival a free event, allowing tens of thousands to attend without tickets. Released the

next spring, the *Woodstock* movie was very long, and served its target audience very well. There was also a three-record soundtrack album which was very successful.

4. Along with the financial success of the movie and the soundtrack, came a certain credibility of the event. This was something that we could look up and study. Despite all the controversies of Woodstock, one thing that is still undisputed is the display of unity and love. Unity was possible because of the prevailing sense of love all over Yasgur's farm. Not even drugs and hedonism could wreck that. In its pure form, love was – and still is – accepting, gracious, kind, and even selfless. (The media has co-opted this for incorrect purposes these days, but that is another discussion.) As an Event, Woodstock demonstrated the power in unity very well, and that is what caught the imagination of the youth, later (sometimes) known as the "Woodstock Generation." What a significant time in History!

Power in Unity

Yes, there is great and effective power in unity. Or should I say "power in numbers"? Is anything worthwhile ever conquered (or achieved) with division? *"Divide and conquer"* is a method of war. If a unit becomes divided during a battle, often they will begin to fight against each other. As the unit becomes weaker, the opposing team will overpower and conquer them.

Somewhere along the line, we have been sold a bill of goods that says that we are in a battle against each other. This is what many would like us to think, especially the Media. The truth (which sets us free) is that people (you and I) are actually on the same team! Yet we rarely hear that, particularly in the Media.

Remember: the Media is all about selling stories and filling time, in order to make money. Oh, they want you to think that they are wide-open and neutral, but they are not. There is a built-in editorial system which picks and chooses subjects. It is very calculated, and surprisingly restricted.

The Big, Bad Secret of the Media

The Media is convinced that only "bad news sells," and that people are not interested in good news. Just a quick glance at today's media, and we can barely believe the sheer volume of bad things that go on around the world. With the advent of 24-hour news (particularly on television, radio and the internet), we see/hear/read more bad news in a week than our parents took in over a full year. The bad news stories on which they focus quickly breeds fear and grief. No wonder so many are depressed!

Yet we know that there is – or there must be – some element of good news and positive news happening somewhere. Once in a while, your TV news person will throw in a light or a positive news story at the very end of the broadcast, but it's usually a cutesy story meant to make you smile for just a few seconds ... while they are setting you up for more bad news.

There are still some good people, some heroes out there, but are they getting much or any coverage? Could you imagine what your day would be like if you heard nothing but good reports and encouragement? I daresay that you could conquer the day with a smile, and probably even look forward to tomorrow. Each morning would be new and fresh, just like the Bible says. A fresh, new morning just waiting on my input and innovation. Much like a blank canvas ready to go, just waiting for today's creation. This is what we should be looking forward to each day.

We do have choices. This is possible, but it takes some effort. 24-hour news is a valid concept on paper, but not the way that it is executed. When the Bible encourages us to *"renew our minds"* (see Romans Chapter 2), it indicates that we have choices on what we allow into our minds. So if we know that most of the Media's news is negative, we should make the choice to not watch it, and to find something more positive to watch/see/read.

"As a man thinks in his heart, so is he."

Believe it or not: I don't have my head in the sand! I understand very well that "life happens." I have a family, and I remember the days we had very little money on which to live. Jay and I married young and started our family immediately, so we only had one income to live on. We didn't dare ask our parents for help as that would mean we couldn't do it on our own. Yes, we had a little bit of pride in that regard. We had a "we can do it ourselves" mentality. Those were difficult times.

The Frugal (Yet Creative) Gourmet

In those early days our food of choice was hamburger and macaroni. Not because we enjoyed it particularly but because it was inexpensive and versatile. There were just so many ways to prepare it! Because we put a little creative style and pizzazz into it, our children were convinced they were getting a new casserole every day.

I learned that all I needed to change the flavor was a can of soup, so we used a lot of Tomato or Cream of Mushroom soup. Hamburger patties and noodles only needed ketchup or soy sauce. Meat loaf was a treat. (Our youngest daughter's favorite meal today is still meat loaf.) Sometimes it was a little hard on Jay and my egos that we couldn't eat steak and lobster as often as we would have preferred, but we did what we had to do to make things work out. We didn't always have a lot, yet we were grateful. We also knew others who had even less. We were just being creative, our children didn't know any differently.

Today we can afford more, and I suspect we may just appreciate certain blessings more because of those early days.

Working Your Own Mindset

"As a man thinks in his heart, so is he." Your mindset is a very powerful thing. A positive thought can begin the construction of a huge idea. The concept of building is referred to in the Bible many times. While every part is important, the most significant single part of building is, of course, the foundation. *"What should our foundation be?"* The Word of God! *"And of what are far too many believers in Jesus ignorant?"* The Word of God!

If we build our minds by renewing them by the Word of God, we will be able to cope. Actually more than cope – we can begin to thrive. Without that foundation of the Word of God, our building will be at least shaky, if able to stand at all.

There is an old Sunday School chorus that seems deceptively simple, but it is golden. It goes like this: *Read your Bible, pray every day And you'll grow, grow, grow.*

Simple. Not necessarily easy, however. Committing to reading your Bible should be a daily discipline, and one of the most important habits we cultivate. *"Oh, the Bible is a big book, and much of it is challenging to understand!"* you say. Well, there are many straight-forward, do-able Bible reading plans available. You can find great books on the subject in Christian bookstores (one of the great secret weapons we should be utilizing), and you also find them online for your smart-phone, tablet or computer. One really easy yet practical way to get into Bible reading is to read "the Proverb of the Day." 28, 30 or 31 days in a calendar-month

– you can just pick the one of that day. An investment of just a few minutes that will really pay off.

Perhaps you know somebody in your church or your city who you see real fruit in their life from cultivating this daily discipline. A living example can be so helpful. It does not have to be another burden at all.

Building Good Towers

We seem to be in the "construction business," one way or the other. According to the Bible, we should be building good towers. We do that by guarding our minds, and getting Godly input. Similarly, entertaining negative thoughts can tear down or destroy our positive "thought towers". Have you ever seen the damage that a wrecking ball can do, and in a surprisingly short period of time? Positive, good, worthy ideas can be demolished very quickly by the negative.

We must be very careful because we don't contain it within ourselves. No, if we decide to "share" that negative thought with another person, we become toxic. Toxicity is not only dangerous, it can be deadly. Sadly, this is often seen at the office (or work environment). There is always one who is never happy, and always has something to complain about. It seems that the complainers never take the issue to management, where a possible solution could be had. No, they complain to people (the rest of the staff) who cannot do anything about it. Do the complainers really want a solution, or do they just enjoy complaining? No wonder morale is down in so many places.

A Sports Analogy: One Pitch at a Time

Let's go to the world of sports. When asked how his baseball team wins so much, I heard one coach say, *"We take it one pitch at a time. That is our focus. Any more than that could get us caught in a downward spiral, and rob of us a victory."* Apparently what he is doing is helping his team get a small victory with every good pitch, building on that, hopefully for a win. This strategy creates agreement and unity for the team.

My exposure to baseball is somewhat limited, but I would have thought that the coaches would have advocated that their team went for the big plays, the more spectacular plays – such as home runs or stealing bases. Apparently not. I have heard it said by the sports experts that the biggest and most important part of winning is not physical ability (though that is also important) – the winner's key is mental preparation (also known as "mindset").

How to Be a Better Singer

This concept adapts nicely to singing. One of the best singing teachers told me: *"Before you sing the note, see and hear the note in your mind."* That was a huge help to me over the years. Concentration (focus) is also a must when singing. In a sense, there seems to be an awful lot to think about: breathing, breaks, ends, sounds, vowels, pronunciation, etc. It can be a lengthy list, and it gets even more complicated when you are in a group: thinking about the others, listening and blending, starting and finishing words and phrases together. If we don't do these things, it will sound terrible. The goal is to sound unified like a group singing together at the same time. And make it look easy ... or at least, relaxed.

Then you get to stand in front of people and sing. This is the time to gather up your nerves, find your confidence and perform in front of the people. Really, this is all mindset. It is essential that we don't give in to doubt, because that is the beginning of a slow, painful descent into embarrassment, a down-ward spiral of no return. *"Oh no! I can't. I just can't. I can't do this. I think I'm going to be sick. Run, run, run away. Oh, nooooo!"*

Some of this is just practice. Most every worthwhile skill requires practice. When I was young and just starting, this was a common script in my mind each time I got up to sing. As I grew in my ability, I realized that the audience wouldn't bite me or hurt me, so I got better. After a while, the nerves were still there – but that actually drove me to excellence, not the fear of failure.

Leading worship is quite a bit more than merely singing. In order to be an effective worship leader, there are several other skills that must be added (but that is another discussion).

The Mindset Is a Key

Having a unified mindset with God makes me unified with Him. This chapter began with a detailed description of what unity can accomplish. We can learn from the lesson of Woodstock, even today. They were there together, they loved and received love without judgment, and they were all basically on the same page.

Unity! Not male against female. Not Country against Rock. Not hip against straight. Unity. Some of you will not like this, but in a way, Woodstock represented a secular version of a worship service. And it taught the world a lesson.

Dare we join together for good in unity today? Can we break down the dividing walls? Can we choose to be positive? Can we operate without the negative beliefs? Our calling today should not be *"divide and conquer"* – it should be **unite** and see the victory!

"As a man thinks in his heart, so is he."

Chapter 8: **Purity**

The Contentment to Be One's Utmost, Authentic Self

"Kelly, what does your heart tell you about purity?"

My girlfriend Carolyn and I were walking our dogs one day, and seemingly out of the blue, she asked me this leading question about purity. First, here is a little background:

We were walking in an "off-leash" Dog Park, which Carolyn had nicknamed "Doggy Disneyland." It was a warm spring day in Calgary, which is not much like those days in Ireland as celebrated by the *Irish Spring* commercials on television (*"Manly, yes, but I like it too!"* Remember?). No, because of the many dogs in the park that day, the smell was certainly "fresh" ... but not in the pleasant way that fresh usually is thought of. The grass was not yet green, very few leaves had begun to appear on the trees and the snow had just begun to melt. Not exactly picture-postcard.

I had my bashful little Lhasa Apso Sophie, and my girlfriend had her buff black Labrador named Kip. Despite the smells, the damp weather and the less-than-inspiring setting, the dogs were having a great run together. Kip and the usually shy Sophie played and jumped and bounced like they had been locked up all winter long.

When Carolyn's unexpected question was asked, it kind of threw me off-balance a bit. My mind was racing with possible responses, but I wasn't quite sure what to say because the question came out of the blue. I opened my mouth to respond – but before I could utter a sound, Carolyn came to the rescue and said that she was planning to write a book about purity. Carolyn was doing research by asking various friends for their opinions on the topic. Hence her question.

I smiled and relaxed. Off the top of my head, I said that my initial thought is that purity had to do with being the purest form of oneself. Most of the time in church, if someone mentions purity, it has to do primarily with moral purity or chastity in the sexual arena. While that is certainly valid (and a much-needed message for believers today), that wasn't my first thought or focus. I mentioned that we needed to take away all the "stuff" and get down to an original, basic form. Purify yourself, if you will.

Carolyn and I continued our conversation for quite a while, discussing various aspects of purity, then we went our separate ways. I took my tired but happy Sophie home. But though the conversation ended, my thinking about purity continued. I wanted to look deeper. This was an important topic.

"This Is Gonna Be the Best Day of My Life!"

Over the next several days, my mind flashed back to that experience in that uninspiring Dog Park. As I recalled what I saw, I looked beyond the surface of the grey, dank environment... and noticed that there were many dogs of all kinds, engaging with each other and playing freely. From the intense way the dogs played together, one might think that it was the best day of their lives, rather than a depressing and imperfect day. These canines were content and pure, just being dogs. They weren't waiting for everything to be perfect: warmer temperatures, clearer skies or more lush grass. No, they were having a good time right then. Those dogs didn't know each other ... and it didn't matter. It was obvious to me that these dogs were not waiting for ideal circumstances to arrive – they just made the most of what they had. They were living in the moment.

Yes, there was a "Purity" of sorts about it. Even among dogs that they didn't know, the dogs had absolutely no difficulty being themselves: sweating and panting, playing with each other happily. It reminded me of a recent, infectious Pop song that has this memorable line in the lyrics: *"This is gonna be the best day of my life."*

Just in case, I looked up the lyrics to this Pop song, and it seems to be mostly about young love and anticipation. Lots of *"wooos"* too, which probably means that the songwriters were so happy that they ran out of words. (I am not sure about this, of course.) Despite what they want you to believe, dogs are not people so things are not exactly the same, yet it was very clear that those dogs in the dog park were living their lives to the full. There was an authenticity to the dogs' behavior. I am pretty sure that the dogs weren't holding back things, or saving anything for a rainy day.

They were living in the now, and enjoying every moment. There was no dog worrying about whether this collar might make her look overweight to the other dogs, no preoccupation with acting cool, no concern about image or reputation. No, just a pure desire to have fun. It was so simple. It was so ... pure.

I have to admit that, in a way, I was a little bit jealous of the dogs. The conversation that Carolyn and I had was about the value and importance of purity – that was good. Amazingly, while we discussed the subject, our dogs were showing us a real-life example of purity in the sense of pure joy! If I hadn't paid attention, I would have missed it. God can speak to us in all kinds of ways.

Of course, we human beings start out much freer than we generally become as adults. All of us have marvelled watching little children play and enjoy every bit of life that they possibly can. They don't have filters – they simply go for it. And we have to keep an eye on them. Oh yes, sometimes they are probably too loud and they can break things, but there are few things to compare with watching joy on a child's face.

Here Is One of My Goals

In this book, you will read about all kinds of things that happened to me: some good, some bad, some fair, some unfair, and so on. You would be correct in believing that I have had lots of challenges and could therefore justify all kinds of issues and problems in my life. Strike up those violins as I tell you in great detail my sordid tale of pain and woe .... No, wait! Jesus has transformed my life and He has done a perfect work in me! Oh, I am not perfect ... yet. But I am growing in that direction. And while I have not had the worst life ever, I have had some serious stuff that was holding me back. *"By the blood of the Lamb and by the word of my testimony"* – this book is a big part of that – *"I have overcome"* and I am learning to walk in victory. Not complete perfection yet, but I am no longer defeated, no longer limited or no longer intimidated, thanks to the magnificent work of my Healer, my Savior and Lord. *"Thank You, Jesus!"*

If it can happen to me, God can certainly do marvellous things for you. Remember: God is no respecter of persons (see Acts 10:34). I can state with certainty that God has good plans for you. He will change your life wonderfully. One of my goals is to inspire and motivate you to believe for supernatural miracles in your life! Yes, you read that correctly: *"I am believing (with you) for some remarkable miracles in **your** life!"*

Our Lord promises us many things, one of which is Abundant Life. Not "an okay life" ... not a "get-by life" ... not even "a mediocre life." No, Abundant Life, with a capital A and a capital L. I am not suggesting that everything will be ideal and that all problems will evaporate. Perfection waits for us in Heaven – but while we are here on Earth, we can move from a defeated, anemic existence of a life, to something full and wonderful, as we understand just how much God loves us and wants to bless us. We have a genuine hope and God who is pulling for us.

Without Wax

Following that revelation in the Dog Park, I had a long, frank conversation with myself about who I was. I have already alluded to my long-term struggle with not being consistent around people. Depending on whom I was with, different versions of Kelly might show up. If you asked two different friends to describe me, their descriptions could sound like two different people. I knew that I wasn't being authentic ... and I decided to change that.

In my times of prayer, meditation and study, I learned some things. Sometimes it's not really learning some new thing – sometimes it is being reminded of something that we hadn't thought about in awhile. Such as, the origion of the word sincere. "

Sincere comes from the Latin language, and it goes back to ancient days when the wealthy citizens in a city had statues of the gods in their homes (we would call these idols today). These statues were carved from marble, which was a pretty lengthy and expensive process. Occasionally, a sculptor might accidentally slip and break off a section of marble, which effectively ruined the statue.

Then some enterprising sculptor found that melted wax could be used to repair the break; after careful application of wax, no one but the sharpest eye could tell that there was wax filling in the breaks in the marble. The only catch was that in the summer time in that part of the world, the weather can get very warm ... and sometimes direct sunlight on the wax repair would melt, and then the limb would fall off again.

The word "sincere" is a combination of *sina* and *cera*: *"sina"* means "without" and *"cera"* means "wax." So, a statue that was advertised as *"sina cera"* meant that it was the real deal. It had a sign on it identifying the statue as pure and whole. No wax fill-ins. No one had done a quickie repair job – this statue was real, without wax. I think that description is beautiful.

This is my desire: to be sincere, to be without wax. Nothing fake or phony. Real and pure.

Step Up

Prizing sincerity has been very important to me because I used to struggle in this area. I would often not present the "real me" but a version of myself that I quickly customized to fit the situation and the people with whom I was with. Abandoning this tendency has taken some time and work, but my commitment is to be real, authentic and sincere. And so I am.

Now I understand that our different friends may bring out certain components of our personality. With some girlfriends who are musical, much of our conversation centers on worship and songs. Other girlfriends excel in the domestic realm, so we discuss children, home and family. Some seem to be all about sports. Politics and elections preoccupy others. Regardless of the topic of the situation, I need to exercise discretion here.

There are differences between some of our friends too: some are believers, and others are secular people. It is very likely that most of my readers will be believers. Believers: I hope you have some non-believers as friends! You will probably not discuss – say, the deep moving of prophetic gifts – with a girlfriend who says she doesn't understand, let alone believe in God. However, the Holy Spirit is also very practical, so you can indeed be multi-faceted, with a number of interests and skills, and still be very true to whom God has called you to be.

The Apostle Paul discussed this "versatility": advising that we should *"become all things to all men, that by some means, we could save some"* (see 1 Corinthians 9:19-23). What we are going for here is being sincere, real, versatile, and flexible. And we can do it all, with God's help and love.

Does that sound like too much for you to achieve? Let's remember that all of us are "works in progress" in the Master's workshop. We serve a powerful yet compassionate God. While our loving Lord does not expect perfection, I think that He does expect reasonable effort and steady improvement as we lean on His wisdom and power. Let's step up and be all that we have been called to be!

Pure Gold

They call it the "gold standard." It is the best that there is. Shining, sparkling gold. It is usually from what those important rings – particularly engagement and wedding rings – are made. It is one of the most valuable substances on Earth today. We all have admired stunning pieces of jewelry made from gold.

The gold standard is borrowed in other arenas (from the Olympics, to the Record Charts, and beyond) to indicate the best, the top. I am intrigued by this world of gold, so I've done a little study.

It All Comes Down to Purity

Getting gold out of the ground is a difficult and expensive process. Mining is a tough business. Once the mineral is obtained, then the process of purification begins. One thing that every goldsmith knows is that the purer the gold, the more valuable it is. A goldsmith spends years learning his trade so that he is an expert in gold. He knows that gold needs to be put under great stress (intense heat) in order to purify it. It is not easy work to do, but the goldsmith is convinced that the final sparkling product is worth all the effort and all that heat. The slag is separated from what is truly valuable.

Similarly, the purer I am as a woman of God, the more valuable I am to my Heavenly Goldsmith, God. He loves me deeply but He desires a much better, much purer, finished version of me, so He allows me to be tested, sometimes by fire. God knows not only what I can be – He is also well aware of the slag in my life, and He helps me get rid of it through various tests of fire. Confession: I can't say that I actually enjoy a fiery trial yet, but I am trusting that my Goldsmith is helping me get to a much purer, much more usable, and a much more beautiful state.

Being pure is a great advantage. First, it pleases God, and that is reason enough to go for it. Second, it means that I have nothing to hide because (most of) the things that held me back have been literally burned off by fire and heat. When I am pure, I don't have to worry about being deficient, so there is nothing that is going to slow me down. Also I know that the Lord is my Helper, Healer, Source, Supply, Comfort, Strength, Peace, and much more. Thank God that in Him, I am pure!

Mirrors

One of the tragedies of the modern world in which we live is that we are all so busy. The sad result is that we have no time for one of the best parts of life: reflection. It takes a decision to stop whatever you are doing and take time to reflect. It takes time to quiet my spirit enough so that I can simply wait on the Lord.

No, our Lord is not a "genie in the bottle" that you rub and He magically appears. Oh, He does want to meet with us and have meaningful conversations with us, but generally He is very low key and usually not very loud. The Bible calls it: *"the still, small voice"* (see 1 Kings 19:11-13). That implies that in our busy, connected, loud, relentless world, that it is fairly easy to miss Him. I believe that is one of the tactics of the enemy: to keep us so busy that we can't take any time to pause and listen for that still, small voice.

Being quiet and listening are almost a lost art. A mirror reflects what is in front of it. If I look into a mirror, I see me. Mirrors don't exaggerate, lie or distort (unless you're at a carnival) – they simply show back what is in front of them. A reflection is honest ... sometimes, really honest. If you are tired or unhappy, the mirror will show that. If you've been adding some weight, the mirror will reflect that too. If you're happy and looking well, the mirror will give that right back to you.

The advertising business has sold all kinds of products (many of which we don't need) because it has created all kinds of discontent. You can hear it now, the carnival barker speaking loudly while chomping on a cigar out of one side of his mouth:
"Step right up, folks. We have everything that you need for a better, happier life. We have yer face cream, yer zit cream, and yer rash cream. We have yer bottles of Dr. Feelgood's tonic medicine that is guaranteed to cure what ails ya, clear up yer skin, help you drop 50 – I said 50 pounds! – and put a kick in yer step and a smile on yer face! Step right up and get yer wallets out. We leave town tonight, and you don't want to miss this limited-time opportunity!" And he grins rather wickedly as simple-minded folks press forward, dollars clutched in their hands.

If I Could Turn Back Time

I know this is a slight exaggeration ... or is it? It reminds me of that song singer-actor Cher sang a few years ago: *"If I Could Turn Back Time."* You know, the thinking: *"If I only knew then what I know now, I would have done this or that so much better and enjoyed myself so much more."* Great hook, lousy thinking. This may be tempting to consider but it is not at all worthwhile to pursue. This – now, today – is it! Life is here and now. There are no "do-overs."

As entertainment, the movie *"Ground Hog Day"* was very funny – but as real life? Not funny at all. *"Does the Bible have anything to say on this subject?"* Well, as a matter of fact, it does.

The Word of God encourages us to reflect – which is to remember and learn from our past, good or bad. You can't change it, but you can learn something from it. This is called "reflection." It is similar to "meditation" but still a bit different. Reflection means remembering with a purpose. There are basically two ways to learn things:

(1) learn what to do; and (2) learn what not to do. Both are effective teachers, but number-one is usually more pleasant. Learning from my mistakes is positive, while living in regret is terrible!

People Can Be Blunt

Sometimes, people can be blunt. One of my joys in recent years were the workshops I taught on leadership. I am told that I don't look my age (which is nice to hear), and one seminar attendee decided to ask me about that. I will refer to him as "Mr. Question." His question was: *"What makes you qualified to teach this course on leadership? You don't look old enough to have that much experience."*

I chuckled and replied, *"Thank you. I mothered three daughters, who turned out to be wonderful women, inside and out."* I paused, and looked him directly in his eyes. "What have you done?" Mr. Question suddenly didn't know what to say. I smiled sweetly. I didn't verbalize it but let me confess what I wanted to say: *"I took a business starting with one employee (me) and I built it to a staff of fifty people. I have been in sales, and my closing rate was 95%."* Yes, I could have said that to him, but I bit my tongue. I didn't need to justify my position. I was confident that I had all the skills, knowledge and experience to teach the heck out of that course (excuse my colorful language).

The Last Laugh

Funny thing is, that as the workshop began, Mr. Question was still a bit dubious about me. Evidently I proved my value because, at the end of the workshop, he approached me again. Mr. Question told me how great the class was, that he was impressed with how current and relevant my information was, and that much of what I said was very thought-provoking. He shook my hand and smiled, and he thanked me. Then Mr. Question he actually followed up! A week or so later, he sent emails with a description of how he had applied what I had taught and its impact on his business.

Considering that Mr. Question started out the day as something of a skeptic, this was gratifying! Being a teacher is a particularly wonderful profession. That could mean Bible teachers ... school teachers, business tutors…all kinds! You know, a good (particularly a Godly) teacher can not merely impact but sometimes even change a student's life. Most of us can think back to one or two special teachers who did so much more than just teach – they opened our minds and hearts. They called us to far more than the course requirements – they stretched our thinking, they inspired us! That is what a good teacher – a good parent, a good Christian – can do for someone.

The Fine Art of Giving Honour

I know a man who is very creative in several disciplines. He is an artist, a writer, a musician, a director, a speaker, a recording producer, a song-writer – he does just about everything in the Performing Arts (except maybe tap-dancing). He gives credit to two school teachers who opened doors for him through creativity in the classroom. One was a Grade Seven teacher in a public school; the other was a Music teacher at the end of high school.

My friend says that one of the greatest joys in his life was to go back to those special teachers thirty years later and thank them for how well they connected with their teaching skills. He honored them publicly at one of his original Musicals.
Afterward, they spoke of how proud they were to see his work. My friend said, *"I think it was important to let these two people know how much they inspired me!"*

If you spend some time thinking about it, I suspect that most of us have at least one, maybe two or three people from the past in our lives who did something special for us back along the way. I think that letting them know that would really honor and encourage them. Let me elaborate.

I believe in giving honor. The Bible tells us to.

"Let the elders who rule well be counted worthy of double honor, especially those who labor in the Word and in doctrine"
(1 Timothy 5:17).

Giving honor is a delicate thing. You can't just honor anyone, not in sincerity. Giving honor has to be real, *"sina cera."*

In our often convoluted world, you have to look for awhile to find someone worthy of honor. Yet they are there. People who make a significant difference ... people who routinely go the extra mile for others ... people who are more interested in helping others succeed than they are in their own success ... people who sacrifice and give of their resources, their talents, of themselves.

This sounds like an accurate description of "Godly parents"! Do you know a couple who might qualify? If you wrote a card expressing your admiration for the wonderful way they have raised their children – do you think that might mean something special?

What Do Honorable People Do?

1. They do the right thing, regardless of how difficult it is or how unpopular it might be in some circles.

2. They give of themselves. They usually don't make a big deal of it, they just get it done.

3. They are looking for people who they can encourage. They know the value of a word well spoken.

4. They invest in people who can't give anything back. They might sponsor an orphan overseas, for example.

5. They don't just talk about their faith, they live it out every day.

I am not talking about commercialized success, or who is named *Time* Magazine's – or worse, *People* Magazine's – "Person of the Year." This is not about looks, wealth, bad behavior, or aspects that are truly surface things. No, we are talking about character.

Have Character ... Don't *Be* a Character

We all have people in our lives who are real characters. They are often outrageous, and keep us entertained with some of their silly antics. While being a character is amusing, I am not talking about that. Rather, I am focusing on those who have real, Biblical, Godly character. People who have character often stay under the radar. Character is not a showy quality, and much of the evidence has to be searched out. I believe the Bible encourages this seeking:

> *"Ask, and it will be given to you;* **seek, and you will find;** *knock, and it will be opened to you"* (Matthew 7:7).

Isn't it interesting? God is seeking for Seekers. You can start with thinking, but you need to get things into **action** by seeking. Seeking is active. What kind of things should we be seeking?

1. The **Knowledge of God.** We want to know Him, not just know about Him.
2. The **Direction of God.** He has a plan for us, but He waits for us to discover it.
3. The **Blessing of God.** He wants to bless us so that we can bless others in turn.
4. The **Comfort of God.** He is a Friend Who is closer than a brother, and He loves us.
5. The **Heart of God.** He wants to give us so much as we become like Him.

This list could go on much longer, but I think you are getting the point. Godly people seek God actively, because that is part of their character.

Remember: finding is reserved for Seekers. We can – yes, we really can! – be more and more like Jesus as we seek His face.

Writing Your Appreciation

I hope I have stirred some memories and triggered some gratitude in your heart toward some people who have enriched your life by lovingly investing in you while you were young and didn't have much to offer. Or you were insecure, or frightened, and somebody showed you the way. Or somebody who hung in there with you while you learned a new skill or completed an important task.

If this resonates with you, then I will ask you to do something.

Action You Can Take

When you want to express gratitude to another person, you will probably be tempted to go to your computer, or phone, or electronic device, and key in a message to send off to them instantly. Please don't! All these communication tools are helpful to us – there is nothing wrong with using technology, but when it comes to expressing gratitude, it is infinitely better to go the old-fashioned way: write out a hand-written one (or, better yet, a letter).
"Why a hand-written note?" Because the recipient is more likely to keep it (forever). Added bonus: a month from now, a year from now, ten years from now, they can pull out that letter and read it again. And feel good all over again.

As you let your words flow, tell your mentor how they inspired you ... how they walked you through unfamiliar things ... how they hung in there with you ... how much they believed in you (when sometimes you didn't believe much in yourself). Since they will likely remember, feel free to go into detail if it is appropriate. Tell them how grateful you are ... how their small investment in you has gone on to enrich others. You may not think you are much of a writer, but really, you don't need to be. With a little prayer and a grateful attitude, I guarantee that the Lord will help you find the words.

If it is appropriate, offer to meet them for a coffee or tea and a follow-up chat. Be sure to pick up the tab. Maybe it will be your turn to listen to them. If you are mailing a letter to someone far away, you might want to put in a *Starbucks* or *Tim Horton's* gift card, just for fun.

Who Are Possible Candidates For Gratitude?

Everyone can make their own list, but possible people might include your parents or step-parents... your grandparents ... that special aunt or uncle ... or your in-laws. Many pastors and worship leaders feel under appreciated, so there are some possibilities. Professional people – such as teachers, doctors, police, and firefighters – could all be worthy candidates. Employers and supervisors for whom you used to work once upon a time ... coaches and counselors often come up on many lists. Truly there are almost endless possibilities! You have lived your own life, so you know who the very special people are who have impacted you. Make it a matter of prayer. God will speak to you, if you ask Him.

You don't have to do this every week, although you just might get into the habit of it. Pick your shots carefully and make someone's day. Go out and buy some blank cards and envelopes, and some stamps, too. Be ready when someone comes to mind.

When Should You Take Action?

As soon as possible! People aren't always going to be around, or available. All of us have lost people whom we missed taking the time to thank or say "I love you." I know that life is busy, but this is very important to do. Seize the day! Most of them will be thrilled ... and it will do you a lot of good too!

(I would love to hear your stories about connecting with people from the past to say thank you to…)

Chapter 9: **Discovering the Truth**

God gives each of His kids a special and customized blend of gifts. Everyone has gifts. If God is Who I believe He is, He has made His choices very carefully of who gets which gifts. Nothing is random, every gift is intentional.

One of the best things that we can ever do, is to be aware of the specific gifts that we have, and to operate in them regularly. In other words, if you have the gift of hospitality, you need to exercise it regularly, as there are many who will benefit from it. If you have the gift of giving, then by all means, get busy giving. You can affect many lives.

Let me clarify something here. Not all of us are called to be apostles, prophets, evangelist, pastors and teachers; but make no mistake, God does have a plan for each of our lives. In addition to what God has already given to us at birth, Holy Spirit also distributes Spiritual Gifts to each believer individually as He wills (1 Corinthians 12:11)

Friendly word of warning: Don't become envious of someone else's gifts. God truly knows what He is doing, and we need to trust in that.

One of the gifts I believe God has given me is the ability to discern. I can see things – better yet, I can see into things, right below the surface. For example as a worship leader, I have seen an increase in people faking it. I have noticed a lot of fake love, of marriages just going through the motions, of pastors just doing a job with zero passion or authenticity. We know there are a lot of these problems outside the church, but lately I have seen it on the increase within the church. You have probably seen this as well. This is serious stuff, and I am very concerned. Let me get specific.

Making Your Own Version of God

The current (2016) generation between ages 27 and 37 years are a particular concern because almost all of them seem very angry with the church. I will refer to them as "young people." They are hurt, frustrated and often complain that they feel manipulated. Who is doing this to them? They say it is the church. Who do they blame? Well, those who still believe in Him, point their fingers at God. Others have dropped out, saying they no longer believe in God, and they are searching into humanism, Eastern Religions or Science; also drugs and alcohol. The wounded seem to combine parts of various faiths in a kind of patch-work belief system that seems to be all about serving themselves and their needs. *"Trust in God?"* Out the window!

Something Critical Is Missing

There is no humbling of yourself ... no asking for forgiveness ... no admission of sin ... no repentance ... no conforming to the Biblical standard. They are no longer interested in serving God but rather having their own "custom god" (with a small g) serving them. They get on the internet and find videos or essays that do two things: (1) they seem to validate their new self-serving belief system; and (2) these messages lead them further astray, convincing themselves that they are the only one truly enlightened. You would hope that the Bible would have something clear to say on this! It does:

But evil men and imposters will grow worse and worse, deceiving and being deceived.
2 Timothy 3:13

This chapter in 2 Timothy gives us a clear warning about the last days on this planet, and the perilous times that will come. I daresay that it doesn't take much of a prophet to see that evidently those perilous times have already arrived! When the Bible wants to send a clear message, it is crystal clear. The list is long, very specific and blunt ... and it sounds exactly like so much of society today:

For men will be lovers of themselves ... lovers of money ... boasters ... proud ... blasphemers ... disobedient to parents ... unthankful ... unloving ... unforgiving ... slanderers ... without self-control ... brutal ... despisers of good ... traitors ... headstrong ... haughty ... lovers of pleasure rather than lovers of God.
2 Timothy 3:2-4

Here is the kicker:

Having a form of godliness but denying its power. And from such people, turn away!
2 Timothy 3:5

How to Respond

This is a clear description and an even clearer directive, complete with an exclamation point: *"from such people, turn away!"* No misinterpreting that, is there? Not a pretty picture, is it?

Yet, what do you do when these are your children? How do you respond when it is your family member who is struggling in this arena?

Verse 5 indicates that part of Godliness is its power to transform. Many younger people today want the "magic" part where miracles happen, but they don't want to take the miracle that God might choose. No, they themselves want to choose what that miracle is. These wounded no longer wish to abide by God's rules, but they prefer a "faith" of their own design. There is no room for God.

God requires that we change, admit things that might be embarrassing and that we must depend on His leadership. Yet many are desiring to be "God" themselves. It is kind of like having sex before marriage: all the pleasure, but none of the responsibility. With the incessant focus on "me" in our contemporary society, this is not really a big surprise. It is another version of "situational ethics," which is defined as follows:

"Takes into account the particular context of an act when evaluating it ethically, rather than judging it according to absolute moral standards."
from ***Wikipedia,*** *"the free encyclopedia"*

The Inescapable Necessity of Faith

Ultimately, these hurting young people want to believe that it is all about them. There is a smug entitlement, of sorts. Somehow, many believed that what was happening at church during times of worship or even times of teaching, was all about them, not God. Is part of the problem that God is invisible? The Bible says that:

> *For we walk by faith, not by sight.*
> 2 Corinthians 5:7

From the way many Christians practice this verse, you would think that it said that *"we walk by sight, not by faith."* But that is not what is says! If God gives to every man the measure of faith, then we can walk this out.

The quest for knowledge is good, up to a point. But we are fooling ourselves if we don't think that having faith – and walking by faith – is an essential part of our Christian life. The world, by contrast, puts a premium on knowledge, and tells us that faith is no longer necessary or is "for the weak." Enlightened people don't need faith, according to the world. While this sounds quite reasonable to the secular mind, it is incorrect. Faith is always a part of the Christian life. *"Does the Bible weigh in on this?"* Indeed it does!

> *But without faith, it is impossible to please God, for he who comes to God must believe that He is and that He is a Rewarder of those who diligently seek Him.*
> Hebrews 11:9

Child-Like Faith

So we will never "outgrow" the need for faith. God requires that we learn to trust Him, all through our lives as believers. In many ways, operating in faith seems easier for new believers. We call this *"child-like faith."* He notes that many of the boldest things achieved for God happen when many believers are very young in their faith. While we all desire to learn and grow, it is probably better for us to operate in "child-like faith," even as we age and mature.

As a seasoned person with much experience in this arena, I need to state that we (leaders) are simply the conduit that God uses. The Lord is gracious to allow us to get the credit for it occasionally, but it is truly all about Him, not us. God desires to use us in ministry, but He certainly does not need us. (Remember that He once spoke through a donkey in the Old Testament; see Numbers 22:28.) Shall we check and see what the Bible says about this issue?

> *Every good gift and every perfect gift is from above, and comes down from the Father of lights, with Whom there is no variation or shadow of turning.*
> James 1:17

Wikipedia refers to absolute moral standard – and that is God, and His Word. We can trust Him, and we can trust His Word. God's Word is both ancient and eternal. It is not influenced or affected by what might be happening in the world. It is whole and complete, and just waiting for us to discover it – the practical truth inside on every page. God's truth will do all that it says it will, and lasting change and blessing can come as a result of a dedicated search of the Bible.

Something Is Working Well ... Something Else is Not At All

I am so grateful for many wonderful para-church ministries that are sharing the full Gospel with everything that they have. I am so proud of believers everywhere when – in times of crisis and emergency – it is Christian organizations that are first (and usually best) to respond. During a crisis, there often seems to be a momentary sense of unity within the Body of Christ.

This is as it should be. While parts of the church are still effective, much of the church seems to be a big part of the problem itself, sad to say. Almost everywhere you look, there is division and lack of unity. The church claims to be God's arm here on Earth, yet we compete with other churches, take them to task publicly and build fences around our own little camp. The strong implication that *"we are the true ones serving God."* - Wrong! You can probably be glad that I am not God! Despite my penchant for compassion and being long-suffering, I would probably get fed up with the ongoing lack of unity and maybe use some thunder and lightning, and mete out some judgement ... perhaps a plague or two.

Ironically, it is only during times of stress and pressure that the Body of Christ seems to rise up and experience a measure of unity. It is a fact that the persecuted church is growing and thriving. With the recent losses and set-backs endured lately within North American governments – and especially the U.S. Supreme Court – who knows if the long-standing free pass the church in North America has enjoyed (and taken for granted) has come to an end? Perhaps we will do better as believers under an increased amount of resistance by society, and possibly eventually persecution. One thing is certain: narcissism and a complete focus on self certainly has not worked!

It is clear that (1) the world isn't working well; and (2) the church isn't doing much better ... so what is to be done?

A Fresh Look

After 25 years being actively involved in the church, my husband Jay and I felt led to take a break. We left "the church in the conventional sense" so that we might better understand what people outside the church thought. Like a person starting a fast for spiritual purposes, or someone going away to a retreat for solitude and reflection, we wanted to re-discover some things about God that somehow got lost along the way. We believed that we needed to be away for a time, in order to hear from God. It was a kind of self-imposed exile in the wilderness.

You know what happens in the wilderness, don't you? The wilderness is where many holy men were stretched and purified – complicated men, like Moses. Jesus Himself had a wilderness experience right at the start of His 3 1/2 years of ministry. The wilderness. That is where some of us get lost, and some of us get found.

Jay and I thank God that we were found!

The Truth, the Whole Truth, and Nothing But the Truth

Have you ever asked God a question and He answered you, just not in the way you expected? This is my story. I was asking God a very big question:

"God, are there any absolute truths anymore?"

I know that is a big one but that was where I was in my life at that point. In a way, I was not sure what I believed anymore. I had been taught one way of thinking all my life ... and very suddenly I am challenged to think a different way. It is one thing to follow teachings that you've adhered to all your life (but perhaps had never honestly thought through) – *it* is quite another to think differently, and to think for yourself. What a concept: think for yourself!

For many years, I found it easier to just accept what I was taught. I did not check it out for myself. Now here I was at a crossroads. I had serious questions. I had to admit that what I believed was, after all, truth ... but not the whole truth. You recall what the court bailiff makes a witness swear to, with your hand on the Bible? *"I promise to tell the truth, the whole truth, and nothing but the truth, so help me, God."* On the surface, *that* pledge sounds redundant, but it is not. All three parts are listed because human beings sometimes tell only part of the truth ... or tell some truth and some things that are not the truth.

As believers in Jesus, we need to realize that we are on a journey. One part of it is our journey to Heaven and the promise of eternal life. Much of our journey is our earthly journey, day to day. We should not expect to be the same people at the end of the journey as we were at the beginning! God is looking for growth, for progress, for change. God is not looking for perfection, although he is perfecting us gradually. He is making us into something beautiful. It is not done instantly, rather it is a process and a life-long journey. God wants us to know the truth, and for the truth to set us free.

I admit that I am not the only person ever to search for the truth. It was fascinating how God met me in my search.

"Come Walk With Me In the Cool of the Evening"

> *Then the man Adam and his wife Eve heard the sound of the LORD God as He was walking in the Garden in the cool of the evening.*
> Genesis 3:8a; paraphrased

A friend invited me to get away to a beautiful ranch in Alberta. I chose this time to find out what God had to say, thinking He was going to speak directly to my "big question." What did I hear?

"Come walk with Me in the cool of the evening." I couldn't get it out of my mind!

I was introduced to this by a Pastor at the ranch; he also served as the Camp Cook. A friendly, helpful servant of a guy, he began telling me about a book he was reading about Adam and Eve. I thought I knew all about these two, but with some study, I discovered that there was a lot of significant things to learn. It was captivating.

Let's go back before the Fall in Genesis. At the end of each day, God would meet with Adam and Eve in the Garden. In the cool of the evening, they would walk together with God and talk. For the two humans, it was time to discuss their day – for God, it was simply time to spend together. God had no agenda. He didn't have a list of changes He wanted Adam to make, or tasks for Eve to perform. God certainly could have made all kinds of positive recommendations, but He didn't. He just wanted to be with them.

Then it hit me: God wants intimate time with me! He wants me to pull away from the business of life, and just be with Him. He loves me and desires my companionship. I may be busy, and have a whole laundry list of prayer requests – but the God of the Universe, my God, wants to spend quality time with me! This was what my wise, smiling pastor/cook friend taught me. God wants just to hang, with me. Amazing!

I learned something else that has been very valuable to me: I could certainly believe and receive what others teach me, but I also need to do my due diligence and check it out for myself. I needed to confirm things with God's written Word. I don't want to be lazy, not about one of the most important parts of my life.

Why is this important? Because we live in such a "connected world" that if we are not diligent and careful, we can easily be prisoners of our own devices. Yes, I am all for knowledge and information – and I use most of the tools everyday to be a better communicator – but the devices are simply tools to be used by you, not tools to use you. I believe God inspired all these wonderful inventions because He is the original Source of creativity. In contrast to the loud, frenetic throb of electronic media, God is asking for a little peaceful quiet time ... to *"come walk with Me in the cool of the evening."*

Yes, I will get to know God very well through listening to anointed messages live, or on radio, television, or podcasts. I did my own study of the Bible – a book that is endlessly new and fascinating as you read it – I had that down as well. That's a part of it. But the part that most of us miss is the intimacy part of the "Moonlight Walk": the quiet time, alone with God, just strolling through Nature, and listening. In our society, practicing the discipline of quiet reflection is not prized or praised, or perhaps even widely done. That is unfortunate. Since we are in – but not of – the world, all the more reason to develop this special relationship.

Ain't Gonna Fight It

Once in awhile, I am still a bit surprised that God (God!) wants this intimacy with me. Yet He does.

I have decided to follow Jesus. No turning back. One of the very best ways I can follow Him is to carve out and protect that intimate time with Him. This is not a secret. Those walks with Him in the cool of the night. During my efforts to explore Him more, I found my answer. His Name is Jesus Christ, and He is my Savior and Lord. The other absolute truth He gave me throughout this journey is; I Am. I Am will always be, doesn't change, remains constant from generation to generation. He is the first and the last, the beginning and the end, always present. More regarding this later.

Every now and then, I just shake my head: I still can't quite understand why Jesus wants such a personal relationship and quiet time with me, but He invites me. I ain't gonna fight it. In fact, the longer we walk together, the more I desire and look forward to those times. I will cooperate with the ways He works in my Life.

He is the Way, the Truth and the Life!

Chapter 10: **Authenticity and the Samaritan Woman**

John Chapter 4

Take a journey with me. We are going back to New Testament times, to a village called Sychar, which was in Samaria. It was right next to Israel; in fact, bordering a field that Jacob had given his son Joseph over a thousand years earlier.

It is important to realize that, though Samaria was a next-door neighbor to Israel, they were very different from each other, and had virtually no communication between the two cultures. The Israelis despised the Samaritans and avoided any contact at all with them; the bad feeling was just as negative going the other way. In the Middle East, racial and cultural divisions are very pronounced (they still are). Which makes the following exchange all the more fascinating.

Although Jesus was well-trained in His Hebrew Theology (a rabbi, Himself), He was bold and regularly challenged the traditions of men. This practice led to many times of trouble for Jesus, particularly with the more orthodox Jews, who seemingly existed to try to be as holy and steeped in religious traditions as was possible. It appears that the Jewish Boat-Rocker is at it again.

An Unlikely Conversation

Jesus was making a long journey back to Galilee from Judea, and He decided to cut through

Samaria on the way. When He arrived in Sychar, He realized how fatigued He was; on the outskirts of the city, He saw "Jacob's Well," which offered both cool water as well as some welcome shade. Jesus was alone – He had sent His disciples on into the city, to buy food. He was resting, leaning up against the Well in the shade.

A Samaritan woman – let's call her "Samantha" – came to the Well to draw water. As was "tradition," she stepped around the Jewish man resting there. Then Jesus asked Samantha if she would be willing to give Him a drink.

Samantha was shocked, pure and simple. She asked, *"How is it that You, being a Jew, ask a drink from me, a Samaritan woman? You Jews have no dealings with us Samaritans, remember? We are Gentiles!"*

Jesus' voice was steady as He answered her, *"If you knew the generosity of God and Who I am, you would be asking Me for a drink ... and I would give you fresh, living water."*

Surprised by his statement, Samantha continued: *"Sir, You don't even have a bucket to draw water with. This Well is very deep. Exactly where are You going to get this 'living water' You speak of? Are You greater than our father Jacob, who dug this Well hundreds of years ago and drank from it himself?"*

Jesus answered her by saying: *"Whoever drinks of this water will thirst again; but whoever drinks of the water that I shall give her will never thirst again. The water I will give her will become in her a fountain of water springing up into everlasting life!"*

Now Samantha had lived quite a life herself, but she was drawn to the strong yet steady way that Jesus spoke to her. He wasn't speaking down to her, and there was something very compelling about this nondescript Jewish traveler. While she didn't quite understand the concept of the *"living water"* the interesting Jewish traveler was talking about, Samantha was intrigued by all this. She gulped and said, *"Sir, give me this water, that I may not thirst, and have to come to the Well all the time for water!"*

The Game Changer

Jesus' gaze was just as steady as His voice. He spoke with a relaxed intensity. He said, *"Go and call your husband, and come here."*

Samantha closed her eyes, sighed and quietly turned her head away. She murmured, *"I have no husband."*

Steadily, Jesus acknowledged, *"You are telling the truth in saying that you have no husband. Actually, you have had five husbands ... and the man you have now is not even your husband. Yes, you said that correctly."*

Now Samantha was amazed and her mouth dropped open. *"How did the Man know that?"* she said softly to herself. *"How did He know that I had five previous husbands, and the current guy hasn't married me yet?"* Clearing her voice, Samantha spoke slowly, *"Sir, I perceive You are a prophet."* She almost giggled at the realization, but Jesus' gaze continued to be steady.

In His relaxed and steady way, Jesus went on to tell her about what real worship is and about worshipping God in Spirit and in Truth. He says that a better time is coming soon, when many of the barriers will be broken down as more people of all backgrounds embrace the truth of God. Salvation will be for more than only the Jews, and it will not be limited to certain places, such as the Temple in Jerusalem.

Samantha continued to drink in everything Jesus told her. Then she blurted out, *"I know the Messiah is coming (Who is called 'Christ')! When He comes, He will tell us all things!"*

It was time. Jesus revealed to her, *"I, Who speak to you, am He."*

Nearly collapsing, Samantha couldn't speak, but her mind was racing: *"Imagine, the Son of God, revealing Himself like that ... to a person like me! All I did was come to the Well to draw water, like I have done dozens – perhaps hundreds – of times before."* This was a routine activity on an ordinary day. Out of the blue, there is the man ... and He identifies Himself as the Messiah.

Suddenly, the Well became crowded as Jesus' disciples returned from the city. In many ways, the disciples were still the same good, rowdy Jewish boys they had always been. They were not impressed when they saw their Master speaking to the Samaritan woman. *"Why are You talking to this Samaritan woman, Lord?"* they grumbled.

"He Told Me All I Ever Did"

Samantha ignored them. She went quickly back into Sychar and found the important men of the city. She exclaimed, *"Come! See a Man Who could read me like a book! He knows everything about me. Could He be the Christ? Drop everything! Come straight to the Well. Everyone has to see this Man!"* She was so excited – and so persuasive – that many quickly followed her back to the Well.

Because of Samantha's sheer enthusiasm, many Samaritans believed in Jesus right on the spot that day. Any revival is a good thing – but it is even more significant when sworn enemies share in the revival. When opposing forces begin to drop their prejudices, you can tell it is a genuine revival.

The Samaritans were serious about this, and they urged Jesus and His team to stay with them for two more days. Over that time, many more believed as Samaria heard the pure Word of God. It was not merely a dramatic transformation, it was a miracle! This is the kind of power that God specializes in.

Later on, several thanked Samantha for encouraging them. *"Now we believe – not because you came and got us, or by what you said – but because we know now that indeed this is the Christ, the Savior of the world!"* Everything had changed. Revival had come to town. Samantha just smiled for joy.

What Else Did Jesus Say?

Jesus actually had quite a lot to say. Jesus identified the human tendency to become overly concerned with locations, traditions and rules. He talked about consistency. Jesus pointed out that many were not consistent in their lives. He offered hope that better days, and better things were coming.

Dear Reader: There are a few themes that I discuss multiple times in this manuscript. One important theme is consistency. The reason I come around to this critical subject again is I realize how essential it is for me – and really, for any believer in Jesus – to be consistent in our daily walk with Him. While we may not execute that perfectly all the time, we will improve with practice and focus. Being consistent is not merely something we *should* do, it is certainly something that we *must* do. This is something that I have had to deal with personally, so I know that we can have victory in this practical arena.

Integrity

Here is one of the most important parts of John Chapter 4. Jesus instructs us to be the same (consistent) both behind closed doors and in public. This is called Integrity. Though one often hears it bandied around, it is not a cheap word. I think a definition is called for.

Google defines "Integrity" as: *1. The quality of being honest and having strong moral principles; moral uprightness. 2. The state of being whole and undivided."* This is a wonderful character quality to have ... and Jesus doesn't just "suggest we look into it" – He **calls** us to integrity.

My Favorite Part

Jesus patiently told Samantha this: *"Whosoever drinks of this water [from the Well] shall thirst again. But whoever drinks of the water that I shall give [her] him* [this is the gift of God, people!] *shall never thirst again. The water that I shall give [her] him shall be in [her] him a well of water springing up into everlasting life. It is a fountain within us!"*

Remember with whom Jesus was dealing here: a woman five times divorced (or widowed, or both), presently living unlawfully with yet another man. At best, she was a used woman. Would you have selected her to be your emissary? Yet, instead of accurately identifying Samantha's sinful and unworthy condition, Jesus amazingly offers signifying grace and divine mercy! In fact, Jesus is offering grace to her *before* He went to the cross. He knows that the *"living water"* of grace – along with divine mercy – can wash away all her sins!

"That Saved a Wretch Like Me"

This is much like the story of the slave-ship owner John Newton coming to Christ. By his own admission, the old slaver wasn't just bad, he was a wretch! The sins John committed were vile, yet he found salvation, forgiveness, cleansing, and hope for the future. If you have not yet had the opportunity to see the great movie *"Amazing Grace"* – detailing the lives of both William Wilberforce and John Newton – make sure you experience it. It is truly an amazing way to spend an evening. No wonder this great old hymn has spoken musically for millions of believers in Jesus Christ. What a vivid example of whom and how our God can save and deliver!

The Well Within You

As we consider the Biblical account of Samantha in John Chapter 4, I am also struck by another fact: this miracle happened at a well. Brilliantly, Jesus presented His spiritual message of drinking *"living water"* with the tangible, practical illustration of water in a well. Drawing water from the well is both literal and symbolic. As a result of my own identification with Samantha, I think a lot about wells and the water that flows from them. And I think that I like fountains even more than wells.

In October 2014, Jay and I went to Europe, spending much of our time in Crete Greece. Yes, International Travel is expensive, but so worthwhile! Before we made the long trip back home to Canada, we wanted to purchase some paintings for our family and friends. As an artistic person, I am quite picky about Art, so I wanted to purchase certain paintings I thought would speak to the folks at home.

Jay was pleased that this part of the art shopping went quite smoothly ... but when it came to the piece that we would take home for our own home – well, that was a little different. Shopping for our print took some time. We spent hours looking and deciding, looking at many gorgeous paintings, yet always going back to one particular painting of a fountain.

After much effort, we (me, with Jay's blessing) finally decided. Originally I had wanted something very bright and bursting with color. This fountain was painted more subtly and the colors were muted. It was still very powerful. It stood by itself, rather majestic, inviting, and with such character. The more you looked at it, the more you noticed. Yes! I had picked the correct one.

After we brought the fountain painting home, I started thinking through this wonderful Scripture passage of John Chapter 4. This fountain painting has become not only the show-piece in our home, but the literal symbol of the foundation of our worship. And that is the cornerstone of this believer's lifestyle!

The Symbol of My Journey

I have already mentioned that early on in our relationship with each other – and with God – one of the first things Jay and I learned was the necessity of being authentic. Being authentic was sometimes challenging for me, particularly as a teenager. Because of many negative things that happened to me, I could certainly defend my feelings and my tendency to "change my image and personality" to suit whatever situation I found myself in. There were other reasons too: problems

with both my fathers ... poor advice from trusted Christian leaders (on how to deal with issues, or rather how not to deal with issues ("just sweep them under the rug"). Like many other
families, our family didn't deal with problems or issues well, if at all. That wasn't healthy for any of us. Particularly me.

Things were hard, but God was still with me. While I continued to make a series of poor decisions over several years, I was so blessed to have one Godly friend who called me up short, and spoke into my life. Thank the Lord for gutsy, Godly friends! They can make all the difference. I was all of 17, but this confrontation was the beginning of a major change in my life. She pointed out that I was the Chameleon and she had seen me repeatedly adapt to whomever dominated any social situation.

I had done this "great pretender" role for far too long, and at great expense to myself and my own integrity. Oh, I had the sad, sad story all right. True, I was married at sixteen, had my first baby at seventeen, yet I was caught up in a whirlwind of shame and disappointment. Of course, a mother with a newborn is one busy girl. I was forced to grow up quickly.

I Make Some Changes

My life was crazy busy, and I was still struggling with the long-term effects of the abuse (which had still not been dealt with). What I was dealing with was challenging enough, but in those days, nobody was trying to help me. It was like the proverbial "elephant in the room" that everybody tries to ignore.

I also thought people were talking about me behind my back. Paranoia never helps anything.
Since no one was speaking up about anything in my life, it was amazing to have someone care enough to be bold and call me out! The changes I needed to implement didn't happen overnight, but they did begin with a realization and agreement on my part. Yes, there was some collateral damage, but my Healer, my Deliverer was with me through it all.

Kelly Alert

We've heard of the "Amber Alert System": where the Public is made aware of some "breaking news" incident with a child, often one who has been kidnapped and is in danger. We do our best to help out, to save lives. Well, I have something of a "Kelly Alert." Believers should be aware that there are many situations where another person near you is in crisis and needs the help of caring people. We don't need to hold a psychological degree to be able to minister love, support, encouragement, prayers, and wisdom to hurting people. Not meaning to be boastful, I do this often when I encounter needy, hurting people. And there are many of them out there.
Sometimes just a hug can work wonders!

I knew I had to make the decision to be raw and authentic. Frankly, it was neither an easy decision nor one quickly made. When I finally made that decision, I found the experience very freeing. Liberating!

Other people didn't see it that way. Some suggested "softening the truth" or not saying anything. For me, it was too late for that! Like a pendulum, I swung from being low-key and passive to being bold and in-your-face. It was likely much tougher on others than it was on me. Although making that transition was difficult, it was very worthwhile in the end.

Too Much For Some

Since the time my friend challenged me to be authentic, several years had passed. We were now attending a different church, and I was involved with the music department. I was being my authentic self – which was a bit overwhelming for some, I'm sure. I was still being open about who I was – including being transparent about my struggles, insecurities and short-comings.

That brand of honesty was hard for many to understand. One well-meaning leader even asked if I needed to talk about these things, implying that I had some deep secrets buried in my life. He was sure that I was hiding something. In those days, dealing effectively and compassionately with struggling saints and imperfect people, was a critical concept the church had yet to discover.

Us Versus Them?

Us: the Believers ... Them: the Unbelievers. Two sides. Polarization. From where did this concept of Us versus Them come? Well, the problem was, there was both ignorance of the Bible, and a lack of accountability. The concept that "the leader is perfect and could therefore show no signs of weakness" is a lie from Satan. The concept of "a leader as a servant" was not taught widely either. We – leaders, followers and everyone in between – are all on the same road to the discovery of who we are and what we are made for. Not understanding this created an unnecessary division between God's people. Visible authenticity from a leader gives great hope to the follower, and hope for a future that we will get through tough times and learn God's ways.

Pegged!

I was pegged! You couldn't see it but a name was branded over my head. Behind my back, my life was discussed, but never to my face. A couple of times, several people were "warned about me." That is a real confidence booster, let me tell you! It hurt me at the time; ironically, this whole thing makes me laugh now. I mean, how much power did they think I had?

The hardest part was that God was continually talking to me, telling me not to respond unkind, but rather to show love and to pray for those (in the church) who stood against me. Our loving Lord told me exactly how to walk through this dark valley. It was a challenge not to defend myself or to retaliate, but God gave me His grace.
I never said a word.

It would not be the last time that I "took the road less traveled" and bit my tongue. At first, biting my tongue was a bit challenging, but – as you know – "practice makes perfect," so I got better at it. Now it is almost second nature, and I don't have to strain over it at all.

It's All About Obedience

It was a sober realization that this war was being fought in the church. I could have better understood it if it had been on the outside, but these attacks were not from where I expected attacks to come from. They were directly from my sisters and brothers. Hey, weren't we supposed to be in the same family, on the same side, the same team? Ironically, I had information about many of those same sisters' and brothers' sins, and I could have easily exposed them; but I deliberately chose not to reveal them. It wasn't my place, and the Lord spoke to me specifically, telling me not to. The Lord assured me He would fight these battles for me.

This was not the directive I was hoping for. I also saw that this was an arena for those individuals themselves to fight their own battles and break through to victory.

Do You Want to Know a Secret?

Here's a powerful little secret for success in the life of a believer: aside from sins of omission, you almost never regret something you didn't say.

There have been times I wish like crazy that I could take back something I did say, or said too soon, but I couldn't. The damage was done. I know there is a time and place for "holy boldness," but discretion is also a Godly virtue that serves us well. This is all part of those famous *"fruit(s) of the Spirit,"* this one being "self-control" mentioned in Galatians 5

Controlling yourself is harder than most of us want to admit that it is; and few are so disciplined that they can pull off self control – and that is within the Body of Christ! The prevailing notion in the Secular World is that there are few valid rules anyway, so feel free to do whatever appeals to you or whatever feels good at any given moment. One of the catch-phrases of way back said: *"If if feels good, do it!"* Like so many popular things from that era, that is really poor thinking.

The Dragon

Was I willing to fight through on this one? No. This was a dragon much too large and powerful, for this little warrior. Dragons are mythical creatures ... except in the Bible. One Enemy Satan is called is the Dragon. Even the *Disney Company* – who usually makes everything kind of cute or non-threatening – will almost always present dragons as the fearsome, reptilian, fire-breathers. Believe it: dragons are not some misunderstood friends – they are our worst nightmares!

To underestimate how dangerous dragons are can be fatal. We have the Greater One living inside of us, but we are not wise to not take dragons seriously. It is easy to almost forget that we are still in a war.

The Armor of God

I understood that most of the *"armor of God"* mentioned in Ephesians 6:10-18 is defensive ... and only one piece (the *"sword of the Spirit"*) is really an offensive weapon. I knew I had to get to know my "armor," my spiritual protection, much better. The Word says: *"Seek, that you may find"* (see Matthew 7:7, Luke 11:9). *"Study to show yourself approved; a workman who does not need to be ashamed"* from lack of study (see 2 Timothy 2:15). The Bible is really good about this, you know! If we want to know or learn something, we have to go after it.

Right before I start reading, I often breathe a prayer asking God to make the Biblical text clear and applicable to me. God delights in doing so. (Why wouldn't He? He's my Dad!)

The Waiting Game

Wearing the full armor of God was what helped me through a lot of that hassle with church people talking behind my back. The persecution was bad enough, but without that spiritual protection – if I didn't put on my armor, the situation would have been much worse. As it was, everything still took a long, long time.

They say that the waiting is the hardest part. It seems that way, doesn't it? David talked candidly about this very frustration in the Psalms. In Psalm 13, he complained to God: *"How long, how long?"*

After enduring ten years of the same kind of marginalization, I finally did see the sins of the leaders exposed. I almost thought that the day of vindication would never come. But it did.

Changes

A lot of water had flowed under that proverbial bridge, of course. Jay and I had left that church and took a break (of sorts) from steadily attending any church, for about five years. As a couple, we left organized religion. We hadn't checked out of our relationship with Jesus, only our weekly attendance in a formal church setting.

Do I recommend leaving? In answering this, I need to be very careful. Whether leaving is something I would recommend, well, that depends on the individual and their relationship with God. I note that more than half of those who leave, fall away from their faith completely and never return. Most people in conflict are better to stay within the formal church framework and work on their issues there. Others, like us, carried on in our commitment to the Lord, and it was actually profitable for us.

However for the most part, no, I wouldn't recommend leaving. While, as the Body of Christ, we all share much in common, our relationship with Jesus is also an individual experience. Part of what we want to do as believers is find the path we are meant to travel on ... and, like "The Pilgrim" in that grand old book *"A Pilgrim's Progress,"* discover the personal and individual lessons He has for us.

I want to underline that while Jay and I did leave the formal church organization, we never left God. Actually we met God in a deeper way. We also developed empathy for those outside the church, feeling some of the rejection that those who left the church earlier felt. We also heard comments about ourselves being "backslidden." Criticism like that was not only unkind but also undeserved.

Yes, we are a tabernacle – meaning "a place of dwelling, a sanctuary" – where Jesus dwells. It is not a physical building; it's our relationship with Him spiritually. Life with Jesus is not limited to being within formal walls. Thinking we are justified in labeling someone who chooses to have sanctuary with Jesus outside of a building is, quite simply, ludicrous. Perhaps if the church always was safe and a sanctuary, some of the wounded and broken would not leave to escape the hurt they feel within the church!

Done Biblically, carefully and appropriately, there is indeed a place for Godly conviction, of course, but the condemnation, harassment and persecution often practiced, is not that. Allow me to be blunt, so much of the abuse done in the church is not Biblical, and is actually stuff that God hates.

Vindication: Admission of Guilt Leads to Forgiveness

God showed us His faithfulness in that, one by one, each of those leaders who had abused us, came back and met with us. They thanked us for being so real and candid with them all those years before. Those broken leaders were so sorry. They acknowledged the damage they knew they had done. They began to cry. We began to cry.

Those former leaders confessed many things that they had said about us behind our backs, and even told us things that we were not aware of. If it had not been done in complete brokenness and sincerity, hearing those offences being listed would have been really painful to realize again. However, the old hymn tells us about *"the soul-cleansing blood of the Lamb,"* and we were not hurt again. It was a complete confession, asking forgiveness and receiving that soul-cleansing process for both parties.

Most of us understand that being violated places limitations even on the innocent parties, as well as on those who are guilty. When things are not right, then we feel very hampered in doing much for the Kingdom of God. All of us felt a great spiritual release. What a wonderful experience for Jay and I to extend grace and forgiveness to our former "enemies." What a blessing to be out from the burden we had been carrying. What a wonderful God we serve!

My Observations

The longer I live, the more I realize how essential it is for "we" believers to know the truth, and be set free by it. I am saddened by the great ignorance on this subject within much of the church. Ignorance is a tricky word, you know. In one sense, it means that a person does not know they are ignorant; in another sense, it could mean they *do* know but they are not paying attention. They are ignoring you.

The first questions should therefore be: *"Are we well with ourselves? It is well with my soul? Is it well – with who I am, how I am to others and to myself? Am I seeking love, acceptance, encouragement, inspiration, forgiveness myself? Do I treat others the way I would like to be treated? Do I extend grace? Do I come to Jesus as I am?"*

These are very important questions for us to ask. Jesus addresses these very questions in John 4:7-26. With that in mind, let's re-read them and take the opportunity to learn. God gives us grace so – among other things – we can be authentic and real. As you have probably learned by now, I am all about being real.

The well within us will spring up living water. Wow! Worship does not mean all happy songs with happy endings. There is some of that, yet the book of Lamentations is all about being real with God. Telling Him our struggles and shortcomings. Crying out for forgiveness and help. Worshipping in spirit and in truth. The living water comes from within us. The fountain within springs up living waters of grace and mercy every time we need it. We have continual, constant access to draw on these living waters, whenever we need it. We serve such a practical God!

I don't know about you, but realizing this gives me such incredible joy! I can hardly contain myself sometimes. *"Spring up, O well, within me!"*

Chapter 11: **Hearing from God**

There is a beautiful Gospel song by Sandra Crouch which starts out:

> *We need to hear from You*
> *We need a word from You*
> *If we don't hear from You*
> *What will we do?*

Isn't that the truth! There is a deep desire within God's children to hear from their Father.

Now, God is quite versatile and there are many ways that God speaks to us His people. Here are a couple of the most frequently used methods:

1. **Through His Word, the Bible.** It fascinates me that one can read the Bible day after day, and if your spirit is open, you can receive fresh revelation and truth every time you read it. So many times historically, Christians have read the Bible and it has seemed dull, out-of-date and irrelevant to their lives ... but with a little effort and focus, any part of the Scripture can come alive and become meaningful. So many of us have sold the Bible short, and that is our loss!

2. **Through Godly, anointed messages.** This is one of the main reasons to continue gathering together to hear God's servants bring us the Word of God in ways that we can understand and apply to our daily lives. Sometimes this is in church, sometimes in a home group, sometimes in a class – really, this can happen almost anywhere! One of the great blessings of our post-electronic age is

that powerful messages can also be heard and received on television, radio, the internet, and through publishing (the printed page).

3. **Through prophecy.** Of these three ways, this is by far the least frequent method. For certain types of messages and in special situations, God may speak to us through some of the spiritual gifts, such as the gift of prophecy. Sadly, this real and legitimate gift has too often been hijacked by less-than-scrupulous people, so understandably there is some controversy and suspicion about prophecy. However, prophecy is still valid and can actually be transformational at times. In this case, the prophecy we received was powerful.

The Prophecy of the Two Paths

It went something like this: *Jay and I were walking down a road, and we came to a fork. Jay saw a sign with split arrows, offering us two options for our consideration. One was a clear, beautiful, paved path; it was a straight path. The second was a winding path with broken glass all over it. The wind was blowing and the weather wasn't pleasant. There was spilled blood along this path where we walked. Eventually, the drops became full footprints, completely blood-stained footprints.*

Both paths would take us to the same destination, so we had to choose which road to take. On the surface, the better road to choose would seem pretty obvious: the straight, clear path. It certainly appeared easier, and much more appealing. Really, tell me who wants to get all cut up and hurt while they walk the path?

I want to tell you how this all played out, but first let me give you a bit of background. Though we were believers, we were still wounded, we were hurt people. It was hurting people that hurt us. Isn't that the way it goes? *"Hurt people hurt people."* Where did this hurt come from? Some hurt came from family ... some came from friends ... and some just came from living life. Ouch!

That wasn't pleasant to realize, but it was easier to accept than the next realization: most of our hurts came from the church, the Body of believers with whom we trusted our lives – and particularly from certain leaders to whom we trusted our lives. We believed in authority, we were committed to authority ... and yet so often it was authority that let us down. Repeatedly.

"What kind of accusations?" Thank you for asking!

The Problem With the Pigeon-Hole

I had been falsely accused. One issue was that I was a strong woman who worshipped with passion. Was I just too bold? Next, I was an individual who evidently didn't look (physically) like some thought I should look at church. Apparently I was not conservative enough, too stylish or attractive to be spiritual. I was called Jezebel! Jezebel, of course, is one of the most wicked, godless and manipulative women in the Bible. Even Christians who don't know much about the

Scripture understand when someone is labeled a Jezebel!

Jezebel was a symbol of evil, of human depravity. Human beings are complex creatures, and we can be quite different one day to the next. In Psalms, it is clear that on some days, David had the capacity to be Godly, joyous and full of praise. On other days, David was very insecure, fearful and full of doubt. So David had at least two sides (he actually had many more). It is categorically wrong (if not cruel) to pigeon-hole someone with an unfair, over-simplified, negative label, and reduce them to a one-dimensional person.

Life Lesson: Just because something shouldn't happen within the body doesn't mean that it doesn't happen. In my case, I was labeled Jezebel.

Why was I being singled out like this? Had I offended someone unintentionally? Was my concern with my appearance some kind of threat? Was my voice too good? Did I seem just a little too confident? Did my ministry somehow undermine the leadership in a way I didn't understand?

I really believe that part of my message is to wake people up to see the truth. Marginalization has to go! Should this happen? No. Does this ever happen in some of our churches today? Sadly, too often.

Question: Can God use an imperfect vessel? Do you really want me to answer that question? The answer is yes. God frequently does use flawed vessels. Why is that? Two reasons:

1. Because functioning in the miraculous and changing people's lives dramatically has a whole lot more to do with God than it does with man. In

fact, on our own merits, none of us are ever holy enough or perfect enough for God to use. God is gracious to use us occasionally. Yet, even knowing this, that should never give anyone license to abuse others, particularly in Jesus' Name! We are all broken, but we can operate in ministry, with calling and accountability.

Here is what many seem to miss: because God will use broken vessels, that means we need to remain as pure and true to Jesus as we can. All of us are simply forgiven sinners. Our gifts are on loan to us. We need to respect that and not fall into the trap that is so easy to fall into.

2. None of us is even close to perfect. If God didn't use imperfect vessels, He wouldn't get anything done at all.

Birds of a Feather: Smoke & Mirrors and Brother Cowboy Boots

Thus, at that time "Smoke & Mirrors" was my first accuser. My second accuser, "Brother Cowboy Boots," was very popular, traveling around North America. Brother Boots also "served" (and I use that term loosely) as a prophet, and over the years, he had built up quite a following. So many are hungry for spiritual direction! There is really a sincere and legitimate desire for the supernatural in many hearts.

This is nothing new, of course. Man has desired to see the supernatural power of God for thousands of years. There is both opportunity as well as responsibility for those who operate in this arena. Remember this: desire is one thing ... desperation is quite another. I have observed that when word-of-mouth spreads about the efficacy of a ministry, it tends to build up the positive components and ignore the negatives.

In fairness to both men, I believe that when they first started out in ministry, they began in sincerity, with pure motivation. They genuinely loved people, and were in the ministry to serve. God saw their hearts, and He used them. Over the years, however, something changed. Perhaps they became weary or distracted; maybe the attention of the crowds of people got to them. Was it the money? Was it the power? Something shifted, something changed. When did they stop being anointed servants and become paid professionals? The service started out fine, I guess. Many wanted a spiritual word, and to his credit, Brother Boots didn't appear to be all that anxious to "perform." When Brother Boots came to me, he wasted no time in calling me out, identifying me as "a Jezebel."

As a long-time worship leader, I understand the importance and dynamics of momentum. Funny how momentum in a group setting can shift very quickly (something Jesus knew a thing or two about). I thought that this was my church and these were my friends. With all that we had gone through together, one would like to think that my friends would be supportive and at least give me the benefit of the doubt. Not so. With one word, dramatically spoken, from Brother Boots, the air became icy with suspicion and judgment was passed. The proverbial pendulum had completely swung the other way. I was shocked!

Exit: Stage Left

Tilt! That did it. I went straight home and told Jay exactly what had happened. Jay was brilliant! First: he believed me and knew that we had been set up; that was important to me. Jay nodded, saying that indeed that was it. No more abuse! We called the church and went to say our goodbyes. As we were leaving, Jay asked why there were so many masks being worn there in the church. The reply was: *"We all wear masks."* (How is that for a non-answer?) We left and never looked back. If there had been dust on the mat at the front door, we would have shaken that off!

Breaking Up Is Hard to Do

How one leaves a home church is a critical thing. If we have been around any length of time, most of us will have left a church, perhaps more than one. I want to distinguish between a couple of things here:

1. Leaving a particular church is not the same as leaving the Body of Christ. Two different church locations are still part of the same Body. So are two different denominations. Some churches are very much defined by who the leader is. If that leader leaves, then people may also exit because the identity of that church was so tied up with that particular leader. While this is not always the case, personality-driven churches are usually not very healthy.

Nepotism (surrounding yourself with relatives or close friends only) is a tricky situation too. While leadership needs to be strong, there is never any place for bullying. It is sad but it is a fact that too many "ministers" are also bullies. Having Spiritual Authority can easily lead to bullying, particularly without any accountability. This is especially a challenge for those who move in the prophetic gifts. All of this points back to the need for both integrity and accountability. Someday, all these bullies and abusers will have to give account to God for what they have done. I would not want to be in their shoes.

2. While we do have a few "forever friends" over our lifetimes, most of us have learned to recognize that certain relationships and situations are only intended for a specific time period, and that moving on is correct and appropriate.

One church I knew had quite a bit of turnover in its congregation. This was of concern to the leadership. A prophetic word was spoken that this particular church was called by God to be a "spiritual hospital." A spiritual hospital is a place where the hurting can come in, be treated gently and effectively, and after some time, many of them will be released. Others may stay long-term, but the pressure to retain "everyone" was taken off. As a spiritual hospital, that church is still thriving today.

3. There are poor ways to leave a church and there are better ways. In our situation, if we were to maintain our integrity, we had little choice. We did the best that we could to make the exit as clean as possible, but it was still messy.

One friend of mine was in a large church for a couple of years. She found little to do; there were hundreds of gifted people already in place. Her family was approached by a smaller, growing assembly who offered many areas of involvement. They met with the pastor of the larger church and explained that – while they held nothing against his church – they felt led to accept the opportunities at the smaller church. With the larger church's pastor's blessing, that family left on good terms, and were used effectively in the smaller church. No scandal, no hurt feelings, no rumours. This is a much better way to leave a church.

In Proverbs 18:16, the Bible says: *"A man's gift makes room for him, and brings him before great men."*

Next Path: More Broken Glass

There is an old saying: *"You can't keep a good man down."* There is a lot of truth in that statement. Certainly it was true back in Genesis, in the life of one of Jacob's sons, Joseph.

When you read that Old Testament story, you find a man who has a long series of unfair, undeserved and harsh things happen to him. Amazingly, Joseph handles all of them with grace and a wonderful confidence in his God. Whatever the crisis or calamity, Joseph just keeps bouncing back and being blessed. Joseph didn't always understand the challenges ... he didn't know why the circumstances were the way they were ... he couldn't figure out why some people treated him so badly ... and he didn't know how long each situation would take to overcome. But Joseph did have an unbreakable commitment to God, and he just kept hanging in, believing that, in God's time and in God's way, he would be vindicated. And Joseph rose above every challenge. Like cream in milk, he kept on rising to the top.

One key in Joseph's lengthy story is that he kept his attitude positive and hopeful – and didn't sink into sin, despite incredible temptations. Joseph remembered his dreams as a youth, and he kept his eye on the prize. This is a great lesson to teach to our children and grandchildren.

While I am not comparing myself to one of the greatest heroes of the Bible, I can certainly relate on several levels. Jay and I joined a new church, and it wasn't long until God began opening doors for us. We became the worship pastors at that assembly. In previous churches, we were always volunteering our time and talents, but this time we were paid for our service. That was a great blessing! More importantly, I wanted to take the worship and music ministry to a higher level. We served the Lord there for around four years and saw the mighty hand of God do many great things.

Struggles Close to Home

During this time, our 19-year-old daughter Natasha got very sick. The disease was called ulcerative colitis, and as she struggled, it was clear that she was getting close to death. We knew that our Natasha was a real fighter. We asked the Lord to spare her life, and, at what seemed like the last hour, that is exactly what He did. *"Thank You, Jesus, our daughter Natasha is healed!"*

I am still grateful as I write this Chapter. It was nothing short of a miracle, and everyone knew it. Today she is married and is doing well. My wonderful daughter Natasha still has struggles with auto-immune disease, but we are grateful that she is alive and is a survivor. (Spoken like a real mother, don't you think?)

It seemed that God was dealing with us by shattering pieces of our faith in Him, and watching how we responded.

Like most grandparents, Jay and I are crazy about our grandchildren. We love every one of them. Our grandson Elijah is a wonderful kid, but he had some real challenges in the physical realm too. At age 10 years, Elijah was diagnosed with Hodgkin's Lymphoma (cancer). This is a very serious disease, and it seemed so completely unfair that our precious Elijah had to deal with it at such a young, tender age.

Many of our friends joined Jay and I as we contended for healing for Elijah. It didn't happen instantly, it took some time, but it was still an undeniable miracle in our family. God showed us His healing power one Sunday night when the husband of Natasha's friend prayed, and God healed our grandson. While we respect medical science and understand that God will heal through doctors on occasion, we knew that our grandson's healing had to come directly from the Lord Himself. Hallelujah!

Jehovah Rapha

In Exodus 15:26, a wonderful aspect to the character and nature of God is identified and named. I recommend that every believer studies the names of God and knowing this is a tremendous faith builder for each of us. In this chapter, God is called *"Jehovah Rapha,"* which means "the LORD our Healer" or "He Who heals us." Since we now understand this, we put our faith in God. Medical science can sometimes help us, but it is essential to understand that God is still our go-to Guy. Many times He has been *Jehovah Rapha* to us.

Observations

Yes, our journey has often been a hard one. The path we chose wasn't by any means easy. I don't think that we intentionally chose this path but God was with us, as our faith in Him was being tested.

As human beings, it is sometimes difficult to put our faith in and believe in someone we can't see. On the other hand (except for those days on the Golf Course), our pastors and leaders are very visible so that is why it is easier to believe in Man than it is to believe in God? Of course, if the man of God is following the Lord diligently, that is good. Godly women and men certainly should lead by example: *"Follow me as I follow Christ."* However, when they are not connected and they are moving in the "confidence of their own flesh" (intellect, talent, charm, etc.), that is when we say: *"Houston, we have a problem."*

None of us are perfect. Even when we mean well, sometimes human beings make mistakes. I understand that. I believe that the call of God for ministry is not a cheap thing, or something to play around with and not take seriously. Some reading this may not agree 100% with what I have stated; that is fine with me.

As far as I am concerned, my job is to inform you, not to make you do anything necessarily. I am here simply to share with you what happened to me. Your journey of faith is just that: your own journey. My purpose is to testify to God's goodness in our lives, and hopefully inspire you to believe God (and not Man) for your own life and needs. God has called me to the Kingdom for such a time as this, and I will be faithful in sharing my message and testimony.

I am hoping that you will be inspired to walk with me. I am thrilled about the many, many answers to prayer that I have received over the years. I believe that God wants to do great things in your life as well. Allow me to be your trusted companion along part of your journey. Together, we will *"speak to this mountain and say, `Be removed and be cast into the sea' and it will be done!"* Amen!

Stay On Track: Maintain Your Focus

We have to maintain our focus. Though we are on the path to something great, if we are not careful, it is easy to get distracted. Our enemy knows that (most of the time) he cannot de-rail us completely, but he can certainly slow us down and reduce our effectiveness by providing distractions.

That enemy will come through the back door and use all kinds of things to throw us off track. Our God and Savior, on the other hand, knows that we can overcome our enemy by the blood of the Lamb (standing strong in our confession of salvation through Jesus Christ, using the authority of His Name) and the word of our testimony (see Revelations 12:11).

While hobbies, entertainment and sports are not necessarily a problem in themselves. However if pursuing them becomes an all-consuming obsession, then these activities can actually become a sin. Moderation may sound like an old-fashioned term, but it is a great thing to have in a believer's life. Our society conspires against not only believers but everyone in providing so much distraction that Mankind hardly knows what is truly important anymore.

Values are skewed as well. We often believe that celebrity, fashion and many insignificant things are really worth our time, energy, and yes, focus. On the surface it may look somewhat attractive or sexy, but when you look beyond the surface, there really ain't much there, baby. Does it really matter how many hits somebody is getting on Twitter, FaceBook, or Instagram (or whatever the latest electronic distraction is) advertising some product? Many of our celebrated so-called heroes haven't really done anything heroic, yet they receive all kinds of accolades and airtime because the media knows that most people have an innate desire to admire heroes. They may be good-looking, charming and entertaining, but is there really any substance there?

Over the years, much of our society (not everyone, but most everyone) has corrupted each generation to: (1) never be satisfied with what they have; (2) want more and more; and (3) cut the throats of others in order to get whatever we lust for. And we blame God? We have put all our eggs in one basket by having more faith in Man than God. Now we need God. We didn't realize what kind of people we were quickly becoming. May God forgive us. We didn't have a clue where we were heading, and what we were doing. Surely we can do better than this. Much better.

A Lonely Road

For prophesy never came by the will of man, but holy men of God spoke as they were moved by the Holy Spirit.   2 Peter 1:21

A few years back, I journeyed through a season of the prophetic. The messages I was given to deliver were for some leadership in my city - Let's call this one, (Leader one). The first message was to come out of hiding, to clean up their act and become both real and transparent. If Satan were going to do this, it would be done harshly, with accusation. In contrast, I was not to expose or humiliate Leader one, but to reveal truth to them personally so they could seek help and make the necessary changes in their lives.

Do you remember the vision I described in chapter four regarding the bird in the bird cage?

You will recall that the door was open and the bird was free, but somehow she couldn't seem to find her way out. Stay with me now: that vision was partnered with another dream I had about Leader Two in my city; let's call him "Leader (Cage)." This man had fallen into adultery.

The dream was unnervingly clear to me: I barged into his office and confronted Leader Cage about what he was doing, slamming my fist down on his desk. Enraged, I told him that it was time to come clean. Although God never identified my friend's name (who was the lady in the bird cage), I could see her face ... and I put two and two together. Let's just call her "Feathers."

God gave me the bird cage vision first in order to forewarn Feathers that it was time for her to go free, thus preparing her for what was about to happen. About a week later, I received the dream about Leader Cage. On the following Saturday, I phoned Feathers and told her about the dream. Feathers was in shock. Carefully, I suggested that she go to her husband and tell him. I would reconnect with her within forty-eight hours, and if Feathers didn't tell her husband, then I would go to Leader Cage and confront him.

That Sunday evening, both Feathers and her husband were in church. After worship was finished, I stepped down from the stage and went right over to them. I hugged her and she began to cry. Feathers tearfully told me that she had confessed to her husband. He then said that he would begin dealing with it on Monday.

I delivered what God gave me to deliver – no more, no less. He did the rest. This was the truth revealed to bring restoration. It was messy. I am still praying for that situation.

Warning Signs

It is essential that we take seriously the spiritual gifts God gives each of us. By now you know how much I enjoy and how much I put into my ministry of worship. Part of maturing is keeping a proper balance in our lives.

Some musicians I know (both Christian and secular) are fanatics about music, and often go to extremes in terms of practice and study. Sometimes this is done at the expense of their families or other relationships, or even their health. As a musician, a songwriter and a worship leader myself, I can easily understand how this can happen.

Often during music, one is transported away from the every-day life to another rapturous dimension. While I so enjoy times with just me and my piano bringing glory to God, I understand that it is not prudent for me to spend 10 to 12 hours a day, 7 days a week, just playing music. God knows that my heart is to worship Him; He also knows I have other roles that must be addressed in my life – such as being a wife, mother and grandmother; along with my secular job as a flight attendant; being a good friend, and several other worthy pursuits. It is possible to have one's heart in the right place yet neglect other essential responsibilities.

God will enable me in every arena of my life, and that includes keeping an appropriate balance.

I can be whole-hearted about worship and ministering to others without leaving Jay or my kids sitting there endlessly while I "do ministry."

Unheard Warnings

> *Brothers and sisters, if someone is caught in a sin, you who live by the Spirit should restore that person gently. But watch yourselves or you also may be tempted.*
> Galatians 6:1

In yet another message, I was led to pray privately for the church leadership. And guess what: I was given a warning for yet another Leader! We'll call him "Leader Three." I understood clearly that he needed to be cautioned, unfortunately due to fear (ugh!), I delivered this word to his wife, but not to him. Why? Because I was concerned what Leader Three might think of me. So I chickened out, and took the safer way of telling his wife.

I learned later that he had gone to another leader in that church and told him that I had misused the prophetic (guilty- I should have taken the word directly to him). Once again the enemy hurled another blow my way, but the truth came out a few years later. The word was correct, the delivery was wrong. Lesson learned.

My Confession

Regrettably, I can attest to this. I clearly remember just before I surrendered to adultery, that God forewarned me too. I even went as far as bringing over a trusted couple to counsel with Jay and me. I told them I was struggling. They tried to help, but I didn't really want to hear from them.

Somehow I gave into the temptation anyway. No, I can't justify what I did or why. One poor, selfish decision led to another. I knew it was wrong, I felt the conviction of the Holy Spirit, but I foolishly and selfishly gave into my flesh. All of us think that somehow we are above the law, exempt from the clearly stated principles of our faith – or that we won't get caught. That was simply a lie ... and I believed the lie.

I paid for that sin big time...going through a humiliating time of confession... then months (years actually) of counseling and recovery. Yes,
it was costly, but God was gracious to us, helping us along the very difficult way. This was not God's best for us at all.

Do not be deceived, God is not mocked; for whatever a man sows, that shall he also reap.
Galatians 6:9

I have learned to take warnings from the Lord seriously. God will forgive, when He is asked. He shows compassion, mercy and grace to the undeserving. Yet there are often consequences to our acts of disobedience. Even in this time of struggle, God did some wonderful things.

One of them was Jay. I am so thankful for the husband that I have! Jay had every right to be hurt and angry. Yet God told him to look at me through

God's eyes instead of his own eyes. How wonderful is that? Jay never exposed me.

He didn't have to – I exposed myself. Better to fall upon the rock than have the rock fall upon you.

Another Vision

I was given a vision of a castle with many beautiful rooms. One room held bountiful treasures. Every kind of treasure from gold to gems to precious jewels were there, and the room was very full. Suddenly in the vision, there was a long procession of people led by a particular leader from my city ("Leader Four"). He proudly walked around the large room, going from display to display, describing the gems in detail. He outlined how he had found these treasures and crafted them to perfection. When Leader Four got to the gold, he described how he had transformed it to the beautiful state it was now in. If you listened to Leader Four's impressive speech, you would be convinced that he owned it all.

The crazy thing is that Leader Four was not the King! Yes, the King had given him a lot of trust to care for the jewels and to keep them safe. Leader Four had the keys to the treasure room, and he had full permission to display the beauty of the vast, impressive treasure. Ownership of the room remained with the King, however. Thus, when the King found out about Leader Four claiming ownership, the King was enraged.

Here is the issue: God wanted Leader Four to love and care for the treasures, but to remember that the treasures are God's. Even though I never did deliver this word, there are great truths in it for all leaders to consider.

"On Earth, As It Is In Heaven"

God doesn't always reveal our weakness to bring us to restoration. Often He will speak in kingdom terms. He speaks things hoped for, not yet seen on Earth. *"Thy Kingdom come, Thy will be done, on Earth as it is in Heaven."* Often the truth comes through a word of encouragement. God sees more than we do, and He has the whole picture. That is why we are wise to trust Him. He sees more completely than we do.

Years ago, during a time of corporate worship, I had a vision. There was a young girl in a wheelchair who suddenly got up and walked. No one touched her, but all began yelling with great joy. No one got up on stage and instructed these people. The healing began in response to the praise and worship. The leader (me) wasn't responsible because all I did was lead the people in praising the Lord. God took control and it was amazing. There is nothing wrong with Godly leaders – and many times they are used by God powerfully – but we don't need any one person, only the Holy Spirit.

There have been many prophetic messages given to me. Some of those have yet to come to fruition. However I am a believer. One message told me that I would be part of ushering in the glory of God. I am not completely clear on what that looks like, but I am on the journey of obedience and discovery. In the meantime, we are worshipping together, building the Holy Temple of God, a dwelling place for His Spirit.

> *"Consequently, you are no longer foreigners and aliens, but fellow citizens with God's people and members of God's household, built on the foundation of the apostles and prophets, with Christ Jesus Himself as the Chief Cornerstone. In Him, the whole building is joined together, and rises to become a holy Temple in the Lord. And in Him you too are being built together to become a dwelling in which God lives by His Spirit."*   *Ephesians 2:19-22*

Coda

Remember that word given to Jay and I about the two paths and the broken glass? That was a clear warning that even though our feet would get bloody and torn, that we were walking the journey according to God's will. We trusted, and He directs our path.

The prophetic voice: simply the voice of truth.

Chapter 12: **Thanks for the Memories**

The Bible spends a lot of time talking about days. The time frame used in Genesis to describe God's creative process is measured in days. On the first day, God created this ... on the second day, God created something else ... and so on. Because human beings are required to re-charge regularly (also known as "sleep"), we put a lot of emphasis on days, both as whole days as well as parts of days.

The parts of the day when we are awake are like an open book waiting to be written upon. This is a really important truth in my life, which I will expand upon.

David knew this truth. *"O LORD, in the morning will I direct my prayer unto Thee and will look up"* says a verse in Psalm 3. *"This is the day that the LORD has made; I will rejoice and be glad in it,"* says another familiar Psalm. *"Weeping may endure for a night but joy comes in the morning,"* says another Psalm.

One of the most important verses to me about days is this:

> *So teach us to number our days that we may apply our hearts to wisdom.*
> *Psalm 90:12*

We can live our lives intentionally, with purpose. This is a choice we can make. Another voice is that we can just float through the day, something like a pinball being batted around in a pinball machine, careening here and there, being bashed from one bat to another, with no direction. In the pinball situation, it is others who force us to go where they choose. It is not much fun, and the experience often hurts. Yet our days can be significant, if that is our choice.

Moment by moment living intentionally, these are words by which I try to live my life by. My journey has not been an easy one nor has it been an unbearable one. When I need a little help, I simply ask Jesus to help me and He is faithful to help. In the big things as well as the moment by moment things.

New-Found Strength

One morning, I woke up with a new step in my stride and a new personal strength. I felt I had turned a corner in my spirit. Going to my computer, I open my email ... and there was a new message from a friend. She passed on some very practical advice from her probate coach. This turned out to be very applicable to my own situation. "Wow!" I thought, "I think I will write my lawyer a letter on this matter right now.

Halfway through my email, I got a phone call from my mom. I explained how I was feeling about everything, feeling really good about my new spiritual backbone, about my leap from doubt to faith, and that I am right now writing this email letter to my lawyer.

Wisely and gently, Mom suggested that I might want to hold off until the following Monday to send that email. "Kelly, first let's just wait and see. If we are not seeing results by Monday, then send the email." I agreed, closed my laptop and went on with my day.

As I mentioned earlier, my best place to pray is in the shower, so I hit the shower. I needed some good, solid time in prayer. As the water cascaded over me, I thanked the Lord that He is always present. As I was being cleansed physically, I was also being cleansed spiritually. I prayed that the Father would heal my unbelief.

Suddenly, Kari Jobe's song, *"I Am Not Alone,"* came to mind, comforting me and reminding me that indeed I am not alone. I asked the Lord for His justice to prevail, and that I would maintain my new-found strength and not cave in. Showers are about cleansing, which is a process that takes some time. By the time I rinse off, I feel clean and new. I had barely stepped out of the shower when I received a phone call from my lawyer. She gave a full explanation of what was happening, and made me an offer. She offered everything that I had so carefully outlined in my un-sent email!

Miracle!

Did you get that? **Everything** I had written in my un-sent email, which my mom had advised me to hold off on sending right then, was now being offered to me. It was playing out in front of me. I smiled as I realized, once again, the power of the written word. Waiting was so worthwhile, because God Himself was working on my behalf.

I realized something else: God had already been on the job for me in this situation. He had started things in motion for me before I prayed.

When I think about it, I seem to have an ongoing dialogue with God about doubt. I wonder if He must shake His Head on a regular basis at me. God gives us many signs and wonders if we are paying attention. Yet how quickly we forget, always asking Him for another sign to manifest and that we can be led by. *"God, heal my unbelief. And my memory!"*

I encourage you to document things like this (prayer requests and answers) in your life, dear Reader. Write them down in your journal. Record them on your phone or iPad. Assuming that you use it, probably one of the best places to write down things is in your Bible. Write it down, in ink. Keep a record. Down the road there will come times and situations in your life where the pain is great, everything seems dark, and where the circumstances are really challenging. You will need to be reminded that *"Jesus Christ is the same yesterday, today and forever"* (Hebrews 13:8) and that He came through for you.

You can also take it a step further: you can share your testimony with others. That is one purpose of this book, actually. In a skeptical world full of confusion and distraction, we can point to the life-changing, miracle-working power of God.

The Vital Importance of Remembering

One of the many great values in reading the Bible is the ongoing series of miracles which are listed and described. It is very difficult to not be really impressed. Right off the top, in Genesis

Chapter 1, there are miracles – large and small – described. Just the fact that God created in the spectacular way that He did should be impressive in anyone's book! Our God is a very versatile Heavenly Father with a seemingly endless arsenal of miracles which He can perform.

Miracles should be landmarks and signposts which we use to remember the goodness of God. Our God doesn't just do one, two or three types of miracles. Why? Because as the Creator, He can create all day long. He never runs out of ideas or opportunities.

Our memories are interesting things. I am amazed when I encounter a baseball (or hockey or football) fan who can list statistics on all kinds of sports topics and players, seemingly at will. Certain plays or games from thirty, forty years ago can be recalled and discussed in detail, like they happened last weekend. Let's not just pick on sports, though. Music aficionados can provide incredibly detailed trivia on all kinds of musical topics. While technology can do some impressive things with computers, this pales compared to what the human mind is capable. The Bible describes this as being

"fearfully and wonderfully made" (Psalm 139:14).

I've been told that even the most educated of us still uses considerably less than 10% of our "brain-power'" ... and yet many of us – most of us! – don't use much of that brain-power at all. Not even a fraction. For the most part, it is fairly easy to sleep-walk through life and use very little brain-power at all. So what happens? Well, unused muscles atrophy, and you could say that a brain is a muscle, in this sense. Use it or lose it. This applies to many other things as well, but we'll stay focused on the memory issue here.

Of course we have lots of company in the "Forgetting God's Blessings Department." Do you recall the Children of Israel wandering in the wilderness for 40 years after leaving Egypt? Do you think that they forgot any miracles? For instance, the parting of the Red Sea was one of the most spectacular miracles of all time ... yet a few days later, the Israelis were complaining to their leader Moses, and asking to go back to Egypt. They had experienced one of the greatest physical miracles ever ... but when they got hungry, they forgot all about God's power.

"How Exactly Do I Do That?"

Why are some things easier to remember than others? That is a very worthwhile study, but not something I am going to delve into here. What is important for this discussion is that we make a cognitive decision to remember the important things. The best way to do that is to ask God for help:

"Lord, help me to discern the important things in my life and to recall them frequently. God, help me not to forget the great things You have done in my life. I ask this in the all-powerful Name of Jesus!"

This has been my frequent prayer. Now I don't always remember every one of the important things every time, but since praying for this, I am so much better at remembering than I used to be! My memory is not yet perfect, but it is steadily getting better. I believe this steady improvement is not only good and also God-honoring. Again: God isn't expecting perfection in us, just steady improvement.

I have known several Godly people who have decided that daily reading, study and memorizing of Scripture is God's calling on their lives. Like a skilled surgeon in an operating theater, a woman of God who knows God's Word and can quote it from memory holds a great advantage in a spiritual struggle. When the pressure is on, when lives are at stake, you don't want to be fumbling through the manual trying to find out what to do. No! You go to the person who knows what to do because they have studied and practiced, and this is familiar to them. As a worship leader, it is essential I know the Scriptures I am singing about, as I lead others.

"But What If I Fail?"

What if you succeed? Just as becoming an expert in any skill, remembering God's blessings will require:

(1) **Time.** We want to build our muscles, improve our aim, learn how to use these weapons. We have to try and try again. Remember: we have the Holy Spirit, Who will enable us.

(2) **Effort.** Building muscles starts by using lighter weights and gradually building up to heavier

weights which require greater strength. It will take some time. Don't be lazy. Do your homework!

(3) **Persistence.** Others may give up and surrender for any number of reasons. We are different: we have our eye on the Prize! We stay focused and persist.

(4) **A Positive, Expectant Attitude.** We believe we will succeed. He made us to succeed.

Is this doable for the average person? Well, first, forget that part about being "average" – each of us are uniquely created by our Heavenly Father, *"fearfully and wonderfully made,"* and God doesn't make junk. So consider yourself "perfectly made to be wonderful!" This is entirely doable **by the power of the Holy Spirit working in and through us.** *"Lord, open our eyes to see the real picture! Help me to look at situations the way You look at them!"*

The Disciples Missed It Too

In the New Testament, Jesus' disciples struggled with this situation. After Jesus had preached on the mountain side, the disciples came to Him, saying that all these people were hungry but there was no food. Jesus performed an amazing miracle of multiplication, and the disciples were able to feed the multitude, with food to spare.

The next day, the same situation manifested: a huge, hungry crowd ... and again, no food available. Jesus to His disciples: *"You just don't get it. Why do you doubt? You just saw Me feed them yesterday. Your own eyes saw it, and yet you still doubt it."* (See Matthew 15 and 16.) Jesus was not being mean or rude to His disciples – He was just observing what was happening. I am convicted by this because this has happened to me. God is not upset with us anymore than He was with the disciples – He longs for us to grow and move on in this area.

Recently, my friend Cheri commented to me how much she admires my faith. She has seen me pray for something one day and receive the very thing that I had prayed for on the very next day. I appreciated her encouragement...but then it hit me: *"How do I forget these things?"* Faith is an incredible gift! I have to remind myself often of the goodness of God in my life. My Lord has been so incredibly faithful in my life.

I have to renew my faith often. One of the ways I do that is by simply blocking out the distractions of life and choosing to focus on Him. The good news is I can do this almost anywhere: in my office, in my bedroom, in the gym, in the shower. God is such a practical God.

> *Therefore, since we are surrounded by such a great cloud of witnesses, let us throw off everything that hinders us and the sin that so easily entangles us. Let us run with perseverance the race marked out for us, fixing our eyes on Jesus, the Author and Perfecter of our faith, Who – for the joy set before Him – endured the cross, scorning its shame, and sat down at the right hand of the Throne of God.*   Hebrews 12:1-2

This magnificent verse is rich with deep meaning. It speaks to me of lightening our load, of stripping off unneeded baggage or weight, so we are not holding ourselves back, enabling us to run better and faster.

I believe in testimony, sharing what we have learned over the years so that others can learn from our lessons. Revelations says that the testimony of Jesus is the spirit of prophecy. Being authentic in sharing how Jesus was with us in our story, and how He got us through helps others to relate and learn. We are the vessel in which His presence dwells. We carry Jesus in every circumstance and situation. I have been in a place of lament for the last few years which is my path of learning. Now I am ready to praise, talk about the victory.

Victory Over Injury

Have you ever had a friendship where you felt it was one-sided? Everything seems to be about the other person. Being there for them, doing what they want to do, how they want to do it. I remember once going shopping with a friend and when we were finished she began to share what she bought...pulling out each item for me to see. I could see the excitement in her eyes, as well as the great deals she came across. I could almost hear that Ikea commercial in my head as she showed me her lute "Start the car, start the car" Not sure if my American readers have seen that commercial but if not, might be a great YouTube venture for you. Where the one-sidedness comes in is when I went to share what I bought, she was done and not interested. Poof, the balloon was popped.

You've Got a Friend

My grandmother used to say; to have a friend we must be a friend. It may sound cliche but if you think about that statement, it makes a lot of sense. No one wants to be around someone that only thinks of themselves.

I was told once by a friend of mine "Kelly your the best at being a friend". It was an awesome thing for someone to say and I really appreciated her telling me that. Later when I was alone and that stinking thinking had room to speak, telling me that was all I was designed for, to be a friend. There are no important legacies about being a great friend. No success stories. I felt this was such a short coming. Not a quality that this world cheers us on about. How does this influence others? I want my life to impact others, everyone has friends. How is this significant or special? A boss of mine used to say that if there was a career in having coffee one on one with people I would make a killing financially. :) Yes Dan, I am still looking for that opportunity.

Being a good friend takes time, effort, love and forgiveness. I make many mistakes and need lots of forgiveness myself; therefore, I understand how to be a good friend. It is simple, really, I give what I would like to receive. Not for the motive of receiving (give to get) but the old saying do unto others as you would have them do unto you.
Let me give you a little glimpse into who I am now...

I am a Jesus feminist, I love Jesus and everyone who meets me finds this out within hmm 10 minutes. As a Flight Attendant, I have learned very quickly how to connect with my co-workers because we are working in close, very close quarters. If we are rubbing each other the wrong way, we are thankful that each pairing is only for a few days, and make the most of it. Most of the time we get along well. From the time I was introduced to Jesus I have been proud to tell others all about Him. He is not a fable or fairytale to me. He is my brother, friend, lover. My dishes may build up on the counter and laundry goes from the dryer to the basket or folded but not into the drawers, all because I would rather build relationships. I would play Barbies on the floor with my daughters and lose track of time. Was I irresponsible just because the final step of doing laundry was left out? No. Was it different than society states it should look like? Yes!

Going through this journey has taught me that to be a disciple means to be a Christ follower. Be in relationship with Him and show others what that looks like. Walk out life with those that have been placed in my life. To love them not condemn them. To be the best friend I can be because Jesus is my best friend. Jesus reflected the Father, we are to reflect Jesus. He calls us friends. Not slaves. He shows us how to live, love and give of ourselves.

We have listened to each other long enough. Sharing our "stories"... the hurts and trials we have gone through over the years. It is time to share Jesus. Share the victories instead of the injury. I am a crier/sensitive, too conservative for the liberals and too liberal for the conservatives.

Our identity is love, we are now called beloved.

Jesus is sharing His relationship with the Father, that it is a unique Father-Son operation, coming out of Father and Son intimacies and knowledge...He asks:

"Are you tired? Worn out? Burned out on religion? Come to me. Get away with me and you'll recover your life. I'll show you how to take a real rest. Walk with me and work with me- watch how I will do it. Learn the unforced rhythms of grace..." Matthew 11:28-30 (The Message Bible)

All that I have gone through has brought me to Him. I have been bruised, battered, rejected and misunderstood even misrepresented. But I still have stars in my eyes for Jesus. He never leaves me nor forsakes me. He is always with us as we learn the unforced rhythms of grace. As the beloved, He waits for us patiently to be with Him. Rest in Him, be in Him.

Do you just go to God with your well thought out list of needs or wants, OR do you come to him as a friend? Just to love you and be loved. He loves you and wants to just be with you. Much like a walk with a friend or lover. He says: *"Come away and walk with me in the cool of the evening."* Being with Him daily builds faith and perseverance naturally. Then we will be that to others. How we are known is by our love!

Love is our identity. Our home.

God doesn't just want to use you. He wants to be with you. Emanuel, God with us. We will do... out of our love for Him, we don't do things for an identity. As we walk with God the natural consequence flow. Love flows out of us. What we do is not our measuring stick or progress report of how spiritual we are. Instead our daily works are a reality of our life. A life he leads. Let it overflow organically, out of a place of divine communion with Him comes a natural progression of growth in our relationship with Jesus. Be! Not do! Rest in who we are in Him, in what He is doing through us.

Jesus explains also the process of making wine and how a grape can't bear fruit by itself it has to be joined to the vine. Jesus is the Vine, we are the branches. Our life without Christ withers and dies. As we are joined with Him, abiding in the Vine, our true being spills over as we connect with Him.

The kingdom of this world looks for accolades and glory for themselves. The word tells us that the kingdoms of this world will pass away. God's Kingdom will last forever and ever. For all eternity. In His upside down kingdom, we give without looking to be noticed, we raise others above ourselves, we give more than we receive, we turn the other cheek, we love those hard to love and accept all into the family. These are the kind, giving and humble ways of our kingdom.

When we feel ridiculous and lost, may we know that we are found in you Jesus and with the people of love! Whether it is important or not in the world standards.

Know Your Enemy

"Well, Kelly, if all this is true, then how come many of us are still stuck? Why do a whole lot of us lead such mediocre lives? Why aren't more of us doing great things for God?"

These are fair questions. There are several answers, but I want to focus on just one answer: many of us simply don't know our enemy. Yes, Jesus is Lord and will help us, but we also need to recognize that the Devil – the enemy of our soul – is doing his best (worst) to stop us, or at least slow us down. How do we know that? The Bible instructs us clearly:

"So that Satan will not outsmart us. For we are familiar with his evil schemes."
2 Corinthians 2:11 (New Living Translation)

The Enemy will try to trip us up at every opportunity. He will pile one stressful thing upon another, until we break. Picture a large vase. Pour water into it, three-quarters full. Then add some rocks. If one too many rocks are added, the water will immediately overflow. When we attempt to do our life without God, one stressful issue can take us over the top. We need to remember Jesus paid the price for us many years ago, on Calvary. On that day, the enemy was also defeated. His power was revoked and his weapons taken.

The only thing he has now is Deception. He will attempt to trip us up. The enemy will try – sometimes convincingly – to get us to believe a lie. If we accept his lie as the truth, he achieves something. His lies initiate fear, and his desire is that we would be his slaves to fear.

Fear: Oh Dear!

The Bible gives us the perfect response when fear comes along:

"Perfect love casts out fear." 1 John 4:18

I heard one of my heroes, Joyce Meyer, say: *"If you're afraid of facing a person or a situation in your life, God's love can help you put your fears to rest."* Would you like to be inspired by something? Read Psalm 18 in the Message translation. It is so amazing! Here is one powerful part:

"I love You, God. You make me strong. God is a Bedrock under my feet, the Castle in which I live, my rescuing Knight. My God, the High Crag where I run for dear life, hiding in the boulders, safe in the granite hideout ..."

This feeds my faith! I know God has got my back. As His daughter, I am loved and protected. He is taking care of me – present tense. That passage gives a picture of a Knight in shining armor, doing battle on my behalf. What more could a girl ask for? I am a romantic ... but more significantly, I am royalty, a princess already rescued by my Father, the King. Doesn't every woman dream about being rescued by a Prince? Jesus is my Prince. He sacrificed His life so I could have eternal life. Does Satan have any chance against our Father and King? No! Who we are is not what defines us – it is Whose we are that defines us! Let me remind us of Whose we are (and this is just a partial list):

He is God, I AM
The King of kings, the Lord of lords
The Almighty, the Everlasting, the All Knowing
The First and the Last,
The Beginning and the End.
He is our Truth, our Light, our Strength
He is our Portion.
He is our Strong and Mighty Tower, our Ever-Present Help in time of need.
He is our Provider, our Healer, our Deliverer,
Our Redeemer, He is Wise, Infinite,
Sovereign, Holy, Faithful, and Pure.
God is Good, He is Grace and Justice, He is Merciful, He is Omnipotent, Omnipresent, Righteous, and Transcendent. God is love!

Those are just some of the things that describe our God. We would do well to remember these qualities.

When we spend time around babies, we notice how quickly they can learn certain things. And we also notice how slowly they learn other things. No one is born hating someone else – hate is a learned behavior. Yet, as babies can learn to hate, they also can be taught to love. Love comes more naturally from the heart, while hate comes from a place of fear. Fear develops from insecurity, which breeds envy and finally produces anger in the heart; on the other hand, love dispels, dissolves and disarms anger.

There is no fear in love. But perfect love drives out fear, because fear has to do with punishment. The one who fears is not made perfect in love.   1 John 4:18; NIV

Get Over It

Often you think everybody is talking about you behind your back. You're not completely sure, but that is what you suspect is happening. There is no proof that anybody is talking about you, but you've already bought into the lie. You are miserable, even if you might not have any reason to be. Jay once confronted me: *"Kelly, not everything is about you! Get over yourself!"* The nerve of that guy! But when I thought about it, it was a true statement. I realized I don't spend time obsessing over others because I am pretty busy dealing with my own life. *"Thanks, honey!"*

Chapter 13: **Testimony**

NAME: Kelly Coray

MEANING: Bright-headed warrior

TALENTS AND PASSION: Speaker... Worshipper ... Author...Flight Attendant

REAL MEANING: Spitfire ... Fighter ... Leader ... Healer ... Change agent ... Boat-Rocker

Have you ever heard the old saying: *"There's more to the picture than meets the eye"*? On the surface, Kelly Coray may appear to be polished and have her life all together, but this lady has gone through more in her lifetime than most do. Kelly's life is an unlikely tale, yet one in which the invisible hand of God is very evident. The intense challenges that she has had to endure would break many, or cause many others to simply give up. But Kelly chose to respond in a different way – a way which is both unusual and yet very human. And so is her story.

I was born and raised in the beautiful city of Calgary, Alberta, Canada ...home of the world-famous Rodeo, the *Calgary Stampede.* I had an amazing mother, her name is Marie. Marie is a wonderful person, yet she had her own challenges in life to deal with.

Sometimes when we are young and we look for love, we don't always make the best choices. Unmarried Marie became pregnant. With me. In an effort to "keep her secret," Marie moved from a small town in the neighboring Province of

Saskatchewan to the big city of Calgary. Her older sister Elaine took her in and provided a safe place for Marie's rather rocky start in adult life. Marie had long dreamed of becoming a nurse, but the years of study required (along with the costs) prevented that, so instead she learned to type and became a secretary.

Once I arrived, Marie worked long hours at her day-job, and spent her evenings with her new baby girl, learning to be a mother. In most ways, she was (and still is) an excellent mother, but Marie was exhausted. This situation lasted until I was seven months old. Then she met a man.

This man appeared to be her "Prince Charming," and soon they were married. His name was Roman, and he was thrilled to have an instant "happy family". I was fortunate that my childhood went rather smoothly until I was around eight years old. This is when alcohol became the daily routine for Roman – more about that in a moment.

The Other Man

One afternoon after a day of learning about adoption in school, I ran home with many questions on my heart. I always knew something was different but could never put my finger on it until this day. I barged into the house, straight to the fridge to pour a glass of milk and plopped myself at the kitchen table. My mom was getting dinner ready. I boldly blurted out the question "was I adopted Mom?" I remember the look on her face; it was of genuine concern with an element of surprise. She looked at me, smiled and asked why

I would think that. I told her what was taught in school that day and I was curious due to the feelings I had over the years. Mom told me we would talk more about it when dad got home, run along and play.

After dad got home we ate dinner like usual and did the dishes. Roman plopped me on his lap and asked me why I thought I was adopted. Well I said, I am different, I have always felt different, not sure why, so I thought I would ask. He smiled and then told me that I was adopted by him, not by my mother, and I do have a different dad out there somewhere. This was a whole lot of information for a little girl to process.

The Turning Point

The turning for me was one Sunday morning when I was out at the park near our home. Back in those days, it was much safer for children to go out to play in their neighborhoods without parental supervision (a far cry from today). Parks have swing sets, and I was swinging. An old yellow Sunday School bus was driving by, picking up children to go to church.

I will never forget the wonderful couple who drove the bus around. His name was Oscar and she was Betty. What they did absolutely changed my life and my future: they offered to take me to church on the bus. I ran home as fast as I could and asked Mom if I could go to church with them that morning. She said, *"Sure, that will be fine."*
If I had been paying closer attention, I would have noticed a little "something" in Marie's eye.

So week after week, Oscar and Betty picked me up, along with a couple dozen others, and took us to Sunday School. Then they brought us home after church. What was ironic was that Oscar used to live in the neighborhood Roman grew up in. Dad said that Oscar himself was quite the drinker in his day. As a child, I was too young to understand God was working in my life ... and in someone else's life, as well.

Segue For a Special Note

I think God may have a special reward or place in Heaven for people like Oscar and Betty! Over the years, I wonder just how many souls have come to Christ because of faithful servants of the Lord like these two? Driving a bus is not an easy job! They are all unpaid volunteers ... they have to get up early every Sunday morning ... the weather can be treacherous ... and the kids can be loud and unpredictable. Yet these Godly warriors are there on the front-lines, usually giving many years of faithful service.

Here is your assignment, dear Reader: Perhaps you have an "Oscar and Betty" in your life. If they are still alive and you can make contact with them, why don't you make special effort to contact them? A simple phone call or a handwritten "Thank You" card or note is such a small payment to offer for someone being so strategic in your life. Yes, there are "Oscars and Bettys" everywhere. If you can, let them know how precious they are.

Years ago, a wonderful song was written, with lyrics that speak beautifully about this very thing. It could easily be a tribute to the Oscars and the Bettys in our lives. It is called *"Thank You For Giving to the Lord"*; it was written by Ray Boltz. Look it up; it will bring tears to your eyes. It is powerful.

Some day I will stand before Jesus. My entrance to Heaven will be based on my own personal decisions of course, but standing over to the right in the grandstands will be at least two special people cheering me on: Oscar and Betty. Today I honor them and the strategic role they played in my life. There are many others who the Lord has used (and is using) in my life, but it was Oscar and Betty who got the ball rolling. I am eternally grateful.

A New Start

Back to my Sunday School story. Mom approved of the positive things she saw in her daughter. Soon, I was asked to sing in a kids production choir at the church. When the Sunday for our performance arrived, I asked my mom to come and see me sing. When she immediately accepted my invitation, my little face just glowed. This meant so much to me.

I thought mom would just come on the bus with me, but no, that morning she insisted on driving me in the family car. My mom was pleased with what was happening with me at church, but she was also touched by the service. She realized that she herself could have a new, clean and personal relationship with God.

Marie had bought into the lies of shame and unworthiness, because she really didn't know any better. When she found out in church what Jesus was really like – and that her life could be completely different – she made the decision to rededicate her life to the Lord.

It wasn't just a special day for me – it was for her as well. Mom was on fire with this new-found repentance. From that Sunday on, the "Two Musketeers" (as we called ourselves) went to church without fail. It was just Mom and I. It was a wonderful, foundational season in our lives.

My father would be at home, "licking his wounds" from whatever happened the evening before – more about him in a moment.

The Two Best Gifts Ever

Sunday School and church was a whole different world for me. I was learning like crazy, swept up in the joy and excitement of the wonderful Bible stories, the great music, the loving teachers, everything. I was learning, having fun and yet felt warm and safe, all at the same time. There was a lot of momentum: Sunday School through the fall, winter, and spring, and Bible Camp in the summer.

One particular moment at Bible Camp stands out for me. An evangelist was speaking to us children, talking in vivid terms about Heaven and Hell, as well as what Jesus had died to provide for us. It was God's gift of love to each of us, and it was free. Along with many others, I was stirred. I felt conviction and I felt attraction to this loving Savior. Moments later, I went down to the front to accept Jesus Christ as my Lord and Savior. I felt His forgiveness just wash all over me, making me new and clean, and happy. The best single decision I have ever made!

I recall being so excited to begin my life journey with Jesus. Like many new converts, I had a lot of zeal. Probably more zeal than wisdom. God – being God, and a wise and loving
Heavenly Father – knew I needed more than just zeal. This is when I was introduced to the third Person of the Trinity, the Holy Spirit. He arrived in my life right in the nick of time.

Jesus is the Master of timing. Being so young, I didn't realize there is a big old world out there, and while there is much good and joy, it is also full of some not-so-nice people and bad experiences. Yet the Holy Spirit was always with me, protecting and directing me, as much as I would allow Him to. When the Lord says that He will never leave us or forsake us, He is making a commitment that He means, and that is not depending on how good or bad our behavioral choices are.

Don't Miss This!

This is a primary reason Christian families need good, solid, practical teaching about how to live life successfully. Without Godly teaching and instruction flowing consistently into our lives, we can set ourselves up for many problems. If we are ignorant and do not know better, we may very well make some sincere, yet costly, painful decisions. This will waste a lot of time, causing heartache that we simply do not need. Practical Godly knowledge can make all the difference!

Every successful athlete will credit his coach for bringing him to his place of success. God bless all those who preach these kinds of messages, who teach Sunday School and lead home groups as they can provide clear, Biblical direction for those who pay attention.

Readers: Even as you read this, the Lord is speaking to some of you. If you are being drawn to the Lord and His Word, this is a good thing and I encourage you to respond. The Lord is placing in you that desire for Him. Act now! Don't put it off. Remember: the Lord is on your side, and pulling for you to succeed. Please write me and tell me what the Lord is doing in your life.

Two Different Influences

The old saying is that opposites attract. With Roman and Marie, there was a degree of truth in that statement. My father liked Rye Whiskey... while my mother preferred milk. He listened to a lot of Country music ... while she listened to mostly Gospel, with a little Charlie Pride thrown in. They had some compatibilities ... and they definitely had some differences.

On cleaning day, Mom would often play the up-tempo music of the Pointer Sisters. She would turn up the music, and cleaning hardly seemed like work. But if Marie had her musical favorites, so did Roman. There was one artist whom my Dad loved above all the others: Elvis Aaron Presley. On Friday or Saturday nights, after he came home from the bar, with a silly smile on his face, my father would crank those old Elvis tunes as loud as he could without blowing the speakers.

Roman especially loved Elvis crooning his ballads. When I was little, I would climb onto his feet and we would dance. Oh, how I loved that! We could dance to Elvis music for what seemed like hours – until Mom came home from her Bible Study. Immediately, the atmosphere would change. I learned quickly that Whiskey and milk do not mix. A pattern soon emerged.

At first, Roman was such a "fun drunk" ... until he passed a certain point in his drinking. Without warning, the alcohol would turn Roman into a mean drunk. Things were no longer fun for anyone.

The Deception of Alcohol

Like so many drinkers, I don't think Roman saw it coming. That is what alcohol is like: it is just so deceptive. It doesn't affect everybody in exactly the same way; some seem able to "hold their liquor" much better than others. Masquerading as a relaxant and social equalizer, alcohol is very deceptive, and ultimately deadly.

Most drinkers don't believe that, or it is difficult for them to think about it while under the influence, so they keep on drinking. Here is what I have learned: just give the alcohol some time. Watch a few lives over a few years, and see if you don't agree with that, ultimately, alcohol is a thief, robbing people of everything of value.

Wine (or other forms of alcohol) is a mocker, intoxicating drink arouses brawling. And whoever is led astray by it is not wise.
                                             Proverbs 20:1

Steadily, things got worse. Drinking only on the weekends morphed to drinking every day, as the addiction took over his life. Mom was concerned, but her plate was already full. She had a new baby boy, as well as an energetic daughter growing up way too fast. Mom was just so busy ... too busy. She meant well, but something had to give – and that turned out to be me.

I had lots of freedom, which meant I was out all the time. These were the days before cell phones made us more accessible, so Mom didn't usually know where I was, who I was with, or what I was doing. As I am confident that you, the Reader, have already understood: I have always been the friendly type, and had the ability to fit into a wide variety of social situations pretty easily. Unwittingly, I also put myself into some dangerous situations.

The Meeting...

All during this time I was still trying to find out who Kelly was. I was searching for my identity, and wanted to know who my biological dad was. One day Roman came in the house, threw a news paper down on the kitchen table and said to me, well Kelly, you said you want to meet your "real dad" now you can, he is in the Calgary jail. I could tell this was a soft spot for Roman. As an adult, I can imagine how he felt, trying to support and protect me all these years, and now having to surrender information that could potentially hurt me. Mom made the necessary arrangements for me to go and meet Kenny, that was his name.

I got dressed in many different outfits that morning. Anticipating the first introduction to my bio dad, I wanted it to be a good first impression. Practicing in the mirror over and over what I would say. Hi, my name is Kelly. Of course my name is Kelly, I can't say that. He already knows that. After reciting my introduction many times, I decided to just wing it. What to wear? I wore my I love Jesus tank top. It was my favorite shirt.

We pulled up to this massive building with really tall fences all around it. I remember the buzzing with each door as we entered one by one, then they would slam shut. One, two, three doors before we entered the room where he was waiting.

The first thing he said to me as I walked in the room, with a huge smile on my face was: "you got my teeth". That happens to be the one thing I hated the most was my crooked teeth. Good thing I am over it now. Later we laughed for years about that first meeting.

Over the years I had run into Kenny at various locations. One time when I was around six, I remember being at the horse races with my mom. I was not aware yet that he was my biological dad. Somehow I found myself away from her and speaking with this man I had never met. I was telling him that he should get a haircut because his hair was too long (the crazy things kids say). When my mother finally found me, she was surprised to see that it was my father that I was talking to.

Years after meeting my bio dad, destiny brought us together once again. I ran into him in downtown Vancouver on New Years Eve where hundreds of thousands of people were gathered. I turned to Jay, my husband, and said: "Wouldn't it be crazy if we ran into Kenny while being here". I knew he lived in BC but due to his involvement with drugs and illegal activity, Jay and I put boundaries in place to protect our children. We had spoken with Kenny letting him know that we would continue contact with him one on one, but that we would monitor his visits with our children until they were older. He understood.

Approximately twenty minutes after I said this to Jay, we turned around and there he was. The crazy thing was Kenny had just said the same thing to a friend that he was with, wouldn't it be crazy to run into Kelly here. Obviously meant to be!

As I had mentioned earlier, Kenny was involved with some shady activities. By the age of sixteen I had witnessed Kenny shoot heroin and cocaine. Then hope came one day when I had the privilege of introducing him to my pastor, Dave Wells.

I received a phone call early one morning from Kenny telling me he had been shot and he needed my help, come quick. I could tell he was on something but I wasn't very educated about hard drugs so I wasn't sure what he was taking. I needed to take someone I could trust with me, so I called my pastor and friend Dave to come along.

That was entertaining to say the least. Kenny told us that he was in town for work, an assassination, (a cleanup). He was shot but couldn't go to the hospital because he would be arrested if he did. The visit went on for about an hour. After wondering if the stories he was telling us were true or not, we decided it was time for us to go. I am sure this insightful introduction to my father enlightened my friend Dave a wee bit more into the life of Kelly...now back to Roman...

Things Got Worse

I understood that Roman's own father was quite the "wild one" himself; and this was Roman's role-model. That may have explained some things, but it did not excuse anything. In defense of my grandpa, I did not know him in this way as he was always wonderful to me and perfect in my eyes.

Roman was something of a contradiction in terms: partly a great guy, who was a good provider, hard worker, and had great insight into life experiences; and yet, because he had not dealt with issues in his own life, became a drunk who was bound by shame and couldn't deal with the consequences of his actions. The addiction soon took over.

I saw the contrast clearly. Mom was polished and put together, pursuing the things of God. Dad was a tin-basher and a bar-scrapper. It was fire and ice ... and they did not mix.

Caught in the Middle

I was now 15, and felt pulled in both directions myself. Children should not have to choose between their parents, but I was learning that people often make choices that they shouldn't have to make. I still loved God, but I had started exploring drinking myself. Addiction to alcohol – or "drunkenness," as the Bible calls it – is a downward spiral. The process may take some time, sometimes years, but it can be a downward spiral nonetheless.

By this point, alcoholics start doing strange, destructive things. Roman had bottles hidden in pretty much every corner of the house and garage. The booze owned Roman; he wasn't in control anymore.

One day after school, I came home and noticed that my father had started drinking early in the day. By now my mom was weary of all this: tired of the arguments, the broken promises, the denial, and the fighting. Marie was fed up, at the end of her rope.

I felt like a mediator between my parents and wanted to be the protector, so I boldly confronted Roman about his excessive drinking. He was shocked because I was so blunt. Roman did not want to hear this. (Marie later described the scene as if two snakes were claiming the same territory.) Our locked gaze was intense and intentional. He was standing his ground... me too I was not backing down. It became a fight, and everybody knows that fighting is not for girls. Roman had underestimated me, and suddenly realized that this little blonde spit-fire was indeed a fighter! But I was still just a teenager, and he was a lot bigger than I was.

It Always Goes Too Far

Even in his inebriated state, Roman remembered some of the *Tae Kwon Do* that he knew ... and when I got in his way, his hand collided with my ear. The blood began to flow. Suddenly, Kelly was down and out. The ambulance was called. Roman was so upset with himself that he was scared sober. One of the paramedics asked if I wanted to press charges but I declined. I knew that the man who hit me and caused me to bleed was not my father – it was the booze that had taken over.

The Penny Drops For Roman

Good news: this incident was a turning point for Roman. It was the wake-up call he needed to make some necessary changes. Roman actually went to church, seeking help from Pastor Ken. My dad found God in a new and tangible way for himself and started counseling.

Although he was very kind and understanding, God arrested Pastor Ken one morning while in prayer for Roman and gave him a very specific and ominous Word: *"If you take another drink, God will take your life."* Roman took that word very seriously. Pastor Ken prayed and took authority over a spirit of alcohol and addiction. Walking out of the church, Roman went straight to a bottle he had secretly stashed in the truck and poured out the contents on the lawn of the church and said: "God you have to be real, I can't do this on my own."

This was a symbolic gesture, but a very important one.

Roman kept his commitment to God and he never drank another drop of alcohol again. It would not be true to state that everything in our lives was perfect or ideal after that, but this was a major turning point. Our home was certainly a different and better place. Roman was sober on my wedding day as he gave me away to my husband, which meant so much to us.

Over the years leading up to Roman's death our family had many opportunities for healing and restoration. Dad and I worked hard to rebuild what had been broken. We eventually found reconciliation. Dad often asked for forgiveness, owning every part of his sin. He became a broken man. Roman learned the importance of owning his own stuff and not justifying himself, which then allowed him to move forward. I forgave him and was able to enjoy quality of life.

Roman was diagnosed with cancer. He was given less than a year to live but was gifted with approximately six years. As a family, we are grateful for the latter years spent with dad. He became a great dad and he was a wonderful grandfather to our children.

A Two-Way Street

God had used a young girl as a catalyst for change. Perhaps it would have been better to have been one of the adults, but I had become the peace-maker in our home. At the time, I was too young to realize all of the implications, but I had played an important role in my Mom coming back to Christ, and a significant part of Dad's spiritual restoration.

In both cases, it was a two-way street, as they also taught me important spiritual principles. When he wasn't under the influence, Roman (unknowingly) had modeled some of my trust in my Heavenly Father by letting me climb up on his feet and dance with him in perfect safety. What a picture of my Heavenly Father taking good care of me! I always felt so secure with my Father carrying me.

In her own way, Mom was just as influential. I learned how to pray from her. There are many valuable things that a Christian mother can teach her children, but learning to pray has to be at the very top of the list. I crack a smile today as I vividly recall those relentless prayers coming from Mother's bedside as she modeled the vital character quality of persistence in the spiritual realm.

One definition that I like for "persistence" is: "Firm or obstinate continuance in a course of action, in spite of difficulty or opposition." Jay and I refer to this as "stick-to-it-ive-ness." Isn't it amazing what God can do in our lives when we ask Him and let Him do it His way?

My Man, Jay

NAME: John Stephen

MEANING: "Yahweh is gracious" ... Crowned forerunner.

TALENTS AND PASSIONS: Worshipper ... Wisdom ... Peace ... Warrior ... Simplicity ... Sees clearly ... Agent of change. (Note: Notice any similarities to my qualities?)

The Wild Road Trip

God is all about the details, and puts things together before we even know about them. Apparently He isn't too fussy about who He uses to get things done sometimes.

A few months before I met Jay, I had a girlfriend named Cheri. We attended a party one night, and met these two young men, Steve and Todd. We seemed to get along just fine ... and the next thing we knew, they were inviting us to go on a road trip with them, back to their home in British Columbia. Their home was in Coquitlam – about 11 or 12 hours from Calgary. They seemed like really nice boys, and this spontaneous trip seemed like a great adventure.

Technically, I was already grounded (from a previous incident). Cheri came over to my house and we quickly (and quietly) packed some clothes into that cheapest form of luggage (a garbage bag). Giggling like teenage girls can do, we threw the bag out of my window. I told my mom that I was walking Cheri to the bus stop; she reminded me that I was grounded, and told me to come straight back home. I nodded, and we left the house, grabbing the garbage bag and away we went.

We walked right past the bus stop, and on to the convenience store where Steve and Todd were waiting for us, smiling. We jumped in their car, and we were gone.

I know what you're thinking. Cheri and I had only met Steve and Todd the night before. How crazy is that? All the mothers reading – particularly those with teenage daughters – are probably shaking their heads. I am shaking my own head! I know it was a boneheaded move, but it really did happen and I have to admit that things get even crazier.

Hour after hour, through both daylight and darkness, we drove and talked for hours, making our way through the mountains, riding with two strangers. No money, no food and (when we arrived) nowhere to sleep. (Todd turned out to be the cousin of my future husband). Finally, Todd took us to his girlfriend's house, and Cheri and I stayed there.

That was only good for one night, so in the morning we had to leave and seek for new housing. The ever-resourceful Todd then remembered his sister was away for the weekend, leaving her place empty, so he took us over there. We now had a roof over our heads, which was great. Now we needed food.

The Adventure Is Over

Cheri and I went to a department store, stole a couple of garments and we walked out. Minutes later, we walked back in and returned them to a dubious clerk, getting a little cash to pay for food. I looked at Cheri, and Cheri looked at me. We both knew that we couldn't keep doing that because it was way too risky. We were young and foolish, but we weren't stupid. Our little, interprovincial joy ride was over.

The young often just go ahead and do things, without thinking things through. They just naively believe that the consequences won't be that bad ... if they even think about consequences at all!

It was also very naive to think my parents would be warm and accepting. "You got yourself out there, you get yourself back." No help from them. They were really angry. We fared better with Cheri's parents: her mom sent us some money to eat, and her stepfather sent us two bus tickets home, and he put in some money for lunch along the way.

Looking back, I really did learn something. God had looked after us as we took some pretty foolish chances, placing ourselves in some dangerous situations. I didn't realize that trusting strangers could have dire consequences. The Lord was good to us and protected us, even when we weren't thinking clearly. We were not evil, we were just self-absorbed and consumed with our own desire for pleasure, we didn't deserve His love and blessing but He gave it anyways. That is the steadfast love of God for you too!

When Kelly Met Jay

It was Christmas Eve 1982. I was only 15. However, I looked a lot older; most people thought I was probably 18. I decided not to tell my 19-year-old boyfriend Jay exactly how old I was, until well into the relationship.

Cheri called me to come over and meet this brother of some friends of ours. His siblings spoke very highly of him, and I was very interested. I took a bus across the city, and when I arrived at the destination, everyone was playing a game of "Pass Out" – it was a drinking game. You are right: some of my friends were pretty carnal, but this dark-haired 19-year-old guy was pretty attractive to me.

Perhaps a bit of Jay's background is in order. Prior to meeting me, Jay had been dabbling in Occult stuff. He was checking out Satanism. Some of his friends had decided to form a Rock and Roll Band. They were really into it, and headed to the library to find some books on all things supernatural, how to harness the power of the supernatural, and how that would help them in forming the band.

The boys in the band checked out a number of books, including Anton LeVey's *"Satanic Bible."* They began to read and perform some of the rituals included there. It was exciting. They began to have visions of the great spiritual things their band would do.

Things escalated quickly until they had formed their own little sect. Jay was chosen as the high priest. It all happened easily and quickly. Jay had a vision of a hologram of Satan sitting in the audience as they played. They hadn't started working on their music, but they certainly had the "spiritual" vision of the band.

Just about the time Jay was exploring this dark, spiritual world, guess who walked in? "Miss Party Girl who is a Christian." Sure, I loved to party, but I was still very much in love with Jesus. I would continue to talk about Him everywhere I went, including clubs and parties. Because of a lack of clear, Biblical teaching, and because I was still pretty young, I never got the concept of keeping Jesus out of my party life. It never crossed my mind that I might give Him a bad name. I do believe that God is perfectly able to defend Himself, and do it well. In those days, Kelly's theme song was: *"I love Jesus and I also love to party!"*

That was the theme of one of our earliest conversations: I spoke about Jesus, and I politely refused to have sex with him that evening. He told me later that that was what "sealed the deal" for him. I was a girl he would be willing to take home to mom.

The Tipping Point

After about a week of dating, I went to his house to visit. Jay's mother answered the door, and directed me downstairs to where he was. He was sitting on the couch. I sat beside him and said, "Hi." No response. Jay was sitting there, but he was not present – he was meditating.

I looked around the room for clues. On the coffee table in front of him was this peculiar book. I picked it up and read the back ... and I dropped it. This book was a "Bible" about Satan, and Satan was the enemy of my soul! Shaking my head, I was freaking out. I grabbed my coat and I started toward the stairs to leave. Then I heard Jay's voice, "Kelly, I didn't hear you come in."

I didn't mince any words. "Of course you didn't! You were too busy dancing with the Devil." I glared at him. "What do you mean?"

I looked him straight in the eye and spoke in a very stern voice. "We serve two different masters, Jay. I will not take part in the master you serve." I turned on my heel and left.

Jay followed me to the door. I took a deep breath and invited him to go to church with me that evening, explaining that we were having a pot-luck dinner. I think it was the prospect of free food that persuaded him to go with me.

Jay was overwhelmed by the peace and joy he experienced that evening. When Christians come through and demonstrate the love of the Lord, it is so wonderful. I continued to talk to him about Jesus, and I made it very clear that I would not continue to date him if he continued his pursuit of Satanism.

He didn't know how difficult this was for me, as I was still really attracted to him. The Holy Spirit was on the job; I knew in my heart that I must take a strong stand. So I did.

The following Wednesday, I invited him to church again. This time it was simply a Bible Study – no food. Jay came with me, which was exciting for me. As we sat in the pew that night, things began to happen. I felt the pew shake as we sat there. It was like a movie. I ignored it, and concentrated on what the pastor had to say. Jay was intense.

When the study concluded, Jay didn't really want to talk about it. He said very little. I took him to his house, and went home myself. I knew something was going on.

Acceleration

About 10:00pm that night, I got a phone call from Jay. He had gone downstairs to his private area, and suddenly he had a visit from what appeared to be a demon. It happened very quickly, and Jay wasn't sure what was going on. The "being" was definitely evil, and gave Jay the very clear message that if he continued to see Kelly, he would lose his life. Then the "being" was gone.

I could tell that this experience had shaken Jay to his core, and his words came very haltingly. I asked him if he was all right, and he muttered that he was having a hard time talking. It was spiritual warfare! Finally Jay blurted out: "How do I get saved?"

That did it! Jay was ready. I was so excited that I could barely think straight myself. I dropped the phone, and yelled up to Mom to pick up the other phone. "Mom, please lead Jay in the Sinner's Prayer!" (I guess once in awhile, a girl needs a little help from her Momma.)

Things started to accelerate. Jay went through extensive times of deliverance, and he grew in the Lord so quickly. I had never seen anyone run with the Gospel like my Jay did after he was saved. The enemy scared him, all right – right into the arms of Jesus Christ! It was full speed ahead.

Nothing was stopping this guy from his destiny in God.

The two of us became radical. We were a team! Soon, we got married and began our family.

Full Speed Ahead, Indeed

Like every other growing believers, we still had to work through some issues and deal with the problems in our lives. We were in need of a Savior, and His forgiveness.

We learned we needed to extend forgiveness to others ourselves. Jesus' sacrifice on Calvary was a complete work, and our guilt was gone. He had already paid the ultimate price for us, and no one could take that away.

Jay and I were born for a God-ordained purpose: (1) we are to love Jesus with our whole hearts; and (2) we are to share Him with others. The rest simply comes naturally along the journey of life as we know it. Our future is *"Your Kingdom come, Your will be done on Earth as it is in Heaven."* We are moving steadily in that direction, and we don't have to search for our "destiny or calling" or even sweat the small stuff. We just live it.

You, the Reader, can enjoy the same kind of life we do. Be the **best you** that you can be.

Chapter 14: **Peeling an Important Onion**

> `...Whoever leads the upright along an evil path, will fall into their own trap, but the blameless will receive a good inheritance...`
> Proverbs 28:10

Where It All Begins...My mother's name is Marie. She is a Prayer Warrior, carrying authority like no one else. I have learned so much from her, not only in the realm of parenting but also in the Spiritual Arena. Mom taught me to pray simply by her example. Some Believers are blessed to have strong, powerful Parents who know God intimately and conduct great transactions in the Holy Spirit. I have had to face my challenges in the Spiritual Realm but one arena in which I have excelled is in that critical realm of Prayer. Why do I say that? Because Mom has always modelled the value of Prayer, particularly in difficult times and especially in times of crisis. I thank the Lord! I can barely describe just how important Mom's Prayers have been, and continue to be, in my life. What a wonderful, practical, ongoing, God-Honouring Blessing!

I remember walking into my Mom's room when I was just a young girl, and finding her kneeling at the side of her bed, weeping and calling out to God with all of her heart. Prayer was our best response for trouble. The harder the trial, the more intently that she would pray. With Prayer being such a normal part of life in our home, I was shown (not told) how to press in when trials came. Like most good mothers, Marie knew exactly how to show me the practicality of Prayer. Someone said this:

'...Prayer, Kelly: it is a bit like making bread. Just like yeast is the key ingredient in baking, prayer is the key ingredient in living life. Try and leave out the key ingredient when baking bread and it becomes hard or flat. Trials are the same. If we leave out prayer, we either fall flat or we become hardened. Kelly, that is no good for anyone. Prayer then, is essential to life....'

In this sense, I am one of 'the blameless (who have) received a good inheritance...' Just like Proverbs 28 tells us. Thanks for such great wisdom.

It Comes Out in Music

Over the last four years I have been drawn to the Father to worship on a daily basis. I do this at my piano. It is not dull or hard for me to do this, rather it just flows out of me. Some days I can become consumed with worship for three or four hours, barely noticing the time. I am not in front of a large audience of people but simply worshipping for an audience of One. Often I will combine prayer while I worship. When I began this journey, I could only play a few basic chords. Over time, I have figured out how to play many chords and my music has become more "musical". You see, I have this teacher who sits with me...

Like many Artists, sometimes I will write a song when I am in need. About eight years ago I was at a very confused and hurt place in my heart, as a result of some things that were happening at the Church. This song was just a message and a melody flowing out of my heart, out of the pain I was struggling with. Who knew that this song would minister so much to me all these years later. Every day I sing this song and it never loses any of its significance to me. It ministers to me deeply every time. The original was later changed to this:

I Will Follow

Be kind to me, I've been kicked around,
I bruise easily, and I'm healing rather slowly.
Rescue me, take what's left of me,
Sacred surgery.

Pick me up, from unsteady ground, that's sinking underneath my feet.
I have faith like a little seed, the mountain firm beneath my feet.

I will follow you
I will follow you

You were kind to me, like you promised me.
Healing finally, and my scars they tell a story.
Victory after injury, through your love for me.

You picked me up from unsteady ground, it was sinking underneath my feet.
I have faith, like a little seed,
The mountains firm beneath my feet.

I will follow you
I will follow you
I will follow you
I will follow you,

I'm tethered to the heart of your will.
(by Kelly Coray, Adam Gill, & Darryl Swart)

It is such a simple song, but it ministers to me and others. Why? Because it comes from a deep place of honesty within my heart. That is what resonates with people every time.

Not only is this my Musical Theme, this song has become my personal Prayer and Declaration. I have decided to follow Jesus Christ, no matter how difficult the trial. I will continue to trust His Word because it has proven to be true. Not just once way back when, but day to day. Coupled with the Word of God, this song and the Bible has been my ever-present help in time of need. A person with a secular mind might think that all this would get stale after awhile, but precisely the opposite is true. I am usually blown away at how perfectly a scripture fits my life today. It is like it was written just for me.

God also does something else that is really amazing: He reminds me of other complimentary scriptures that I can also apply to whatever situation I am facing. How cool is that? Let me encourage you with a suggestion.

God is a generous Father, and He sees to it that we all have multiple gifts. Perhaps your gifts are not that of Leading Music, Writing or Speaking. Remember this: When he passes out various gifts to His children, God knows exactly what He is doing. Though some gifts are on display in more of a public way than other gifts, no one got all the best gifts and everyone can be used of God to bless others. If you know which gifts God has given you, terrific, keep sharing those gifts and operating in what you have been called to. On the other hand, if you don't know what your gifts are, or are just not sure, make this a Priority for the next 6 months in your life. The Bible says in Matthew: "....seek and you shall find...".

That is a promise from God: if you seek, you will find. To discover exactly what your combination of gifts are, you may have to do a bit of work, and invest some time in Prayer. Not only do you need to know what your gifts are, the Body of Christ is waiting for you to start moving in your gifts. Perhaps you may wish to consult a Godly Pastor, or Counselor, someone who has both an interest in you and knowledge of you. Ask them what they see in you. They may notice something that you haven't.

No More Masks

Jay and I were eventually fed up with the leadership of our church. Everywhere we looked, it seemed that all we saw was people wearing masks. Earlier I mentioned a conversation with our pastor where we simply asked him: 'Is anyone real?' His response was very telling: 'Doesn't everyone wear masks?' Our reply: 'Ummm No. With Jay and I, what you see is what you get.' The Pastor smiled a half smile and shook his head slightly, as if to say: 'Hmmm. You will learn.' Oh, we learned all right. We learned that it was time to get out of Dodge. And we did.

What had we learned? For one thing we learned that freedom meant breaking out. We had been involved in, and watched the church for over 37 years. It was obvious that a few things needed to change. One was the marginalization that we saw. By what measuring stick do we write our margins? It seems that success is measured strictly by the outward appearance. If we look okay on the outside, on the surface, then that is acceptable.

What does God's Word say? According to the Bible, some things that are done are to be done in secret. What are some of those things? Prayer, worship, fasting, giving money, doing good deeds… and that is only the beginning of the list. Why should this be done in secret? Because the more important thing is what God sees in us, not about what others might think of us. A significant difference.

Let's check this out.

Secret Agent

Note the phrase: 'Then your Father, who sees what is done in secret, will reward you.'

Prayer. Matthew 6:5 '..And when you pray, do not be like the hypocrites, for they love to pray standing in the synagogues and on the street corners, to be seen. Truly I tell you: they have received their reward in full. But when you pray, go into your room, close the door and pray to your Father, who is unseen. Then, your Father, who sees what is done in secret, will reward you.'

Fasting. Matthew 6:18 '…so that it will not be obvious to others that you are fasting; and your Father, who sees what is done in secret, will reward you.'

Giving. Matthew 6:4 '...so when you give to the needy, do not let your left hand know what your right hand is doing, so that your giving may be in secret. Then your Father, who sees what is done in secret, will reward you.

Worship. This is much more than singing in a church on a Sunday, this is a lifestyle. Worship encompasses all of the above, meaning that our prayer is worship, our fasting is worship, and our giving is too. Worship is how we live our lives every day. We are in the world, but not of the world.

To See or Not To See

The conclusion that we come to is that it is more about what people don't see than it is what they can see. We walk by faith and not by sight. Bottom line is that if we remain quiet and not blow our own horn, then He will reward us. If we decide to base our success strictly on what we see or hear, our reward will only be an earthly reward while we are here on earth. I suspect that what God will give us as a reward will be far greater than anything we could receive here on earth.

Instead of being Heavenly-minded, we may become too earthly-minded. It is so easy to do too, particularly when we lose sight of the fact that we are spirit first, then flesh. Our spirit will live on forever, meaning that an earthly reward is finished and gone when we leave this planet. As parents, as friends, as Believers, we all really need to be continuously encouraging others to think in the more subtle spiritual terms, not the obvious and carnal earthly terms.

Being Religious Vs. Being Spiritual

It is so important that our Spiritual Focus be God-directed, and not a product of our own design. When Jesus walked on the earth, the group that He addressed with correction the most frequently were the 'Religious' people, the Pharisees and the Sadducees.

Pharisees: Members of an ancient Jewish sect, distinguished by their strict (almost fanatical) observance of the Traditional and Written Law. They were commonly held to have pretensions of superior sanctity. (Google)

Sadducees: Members of a Jewish sect or party at the time of Christ. They denied the Resurrection of the dead, the existence of Spirits, the obligation of the Jewish Oral Tradition, and (in contrast to the Pharisees) the acceptance of the Written Law alone. (Google)

So, Jesus Himself had to deal with the religious extremes in his day. One would think that others with strong religious beliefs would be allies against the world, but that isn't true. You should be ready; many of your greatest battles will come from other religious people. One of the problems with religious people (and there are many) is that they usually have a self-righteous, if not superior, attitude toward everyone else. Why do you think that Jesus (and other teachers in the Bible) emphasizes that humility, gentleness, kindness and love are essential virtues for us?

How do we feel when we are around the self-righteous? Do we feel encouraged or uplifted? Do they make us feel unworthy, rejected and not good enough? We don't like people that try to make us feel that way, so why would we want to be that way to others?

Does that reflect Jesus? Is that being Christ to others? No, not at all. If it doesn't, then we should stop it. In fact, if I feel the need to prove that I am right and I need to let others know things that they do not know, then I am being a self-righteous person myself. Ouch!

Note from Kelly: Always trying to be right is highly over-rated.

The Gift of Friendship

A few months after our grandson was diagnosed with cancer, a good friend of mine (Donna Hope) gave me a gift. It was a book with scriptures regarding healing throughout the Bible. It was incredible how much the Bible talks about the subject of Healing in its pages. This little book became very encouraging to me, and I learned a new level of trust with my Heavenly Father. I learned to surrender my grandson to my Father and trust that He would take care of him. He did. This book has become a vital part of my everyday prayers for my family and friends. Some complain that it is hard to pray, but, when I have the Word of God at my fingertips, it is easy. I am simply reminding God of what He has already said. How empowering is that?

Donna is a woman of God herself. She has a gentle way, she is a great listener and she has a smile that can light up a room. Donna may have spent time praying about how she could possibly help me, but the main thing is that when she saw the book, Donna thought of me and my situation. She bought the book and gave it to me. Donna prayed that it would help me. It did help me, and far more than she probably thought it could.
Side Note: a good friend will do many things in our lives. Here is my Top Ten List:

The Top Ten List of a Good Friend's Qualities

1) Good friends listen to us. Often they have heard us say it before, and they still hang in there with us.

2) Good friends give us the gift of wisdom, and they provide an objective point of view to a problem that we are struggling with. They give their advice gently, not harshly.

3) Good friends remind us to laugh, and not always take ourselves so seriously. Sometimes they will even act wacky, just so they can see us smile or laugh.

4) When it is needed, good friends provide a shoulder to cry on.

5) Good friends pray for us.

6) Good friends don't betray us, They keep confidences, when asked.

7) Good friends make themselves available to you. All of us are busy, and have many things to do, but the gift of time is one of the greatest gifts of all.

8) Good friends give us good gifts. It is not about the monetary value, but a well-chosen book, CD or DVD, or baby-sitting while I have an evening out, this will speak volumes. Just like Donna did. Or simply the gift of forgiveness.

9) Good friends give you room, but they will lovingly call you out, on sins in your life. This is called speaking the Truth, in love, and a good friend cares enough to do it, carefully.

10) Good friends don't keep score. They hardly notice when you disappoint or hurt them. They applaud your success. They are in it for the long haul.

On the surface this might seem a formidable list, but rest assured every point is very doable. You can have this kind of friend. You can be this kind of friend. This list is more about the 'doing' part of friendship than just the 'being' part of things.

Making a Prayer

One of the great things about the Christian Faith is that God really wants to have a personal relationship with each of us. In my case, He knows that I am a Creative type and that things within the Arts, particularly Music, will often speak to me.

One time while working I had a layover in Vancouver, British Columbia. At my hotel, I felt I should pull up a song that I had heard recently and really felt connected to. This amazing song is called 'Oceans (Where Feet May Fail)' and it was written by three writers from Hillsong United, based in Australia. I began listening to it while laying on the bed, pressing repeat so that I could 'bathe' in the song. 'Oceans' is very ethereal, and it has a very deep meaning and I was relating to it in a very deep way myself. It didn't take long to memorize, as it was engraved on my soul quickly.

I decided to take a shower. You will recall that I have many of my best prayer times in the shower. As the water cascaded over me in the physical realm, so the anointing cascaded over me in the spiritual realm. I sang out loud the bridge:
'Spirit lead me where my trust is without borders,
Let me walk upon the waters where ever you will call me. Take me deeper than my feet could ever wander, and my faith will be made stronger,
In the Presence of my Savior…'

In the shower I sang this over and over again, and at the top of my lungs. I was recklessly abandoned, all in! I am sure that the maids working in the next room could certainly hear me.
I didn't care! I have never quite felt the emotions or God's Presence the same as I did that day in that hotel shower. It was like I made a decree between myself and God. I knew that what I was singing
was very serious and not to be taken lightly. Yet I was completely willing to make this commitment to my Maker. Take me deeper…

How many of us make these decrees with God, and with the passing of a few years, we almost forget about it. Then something comes to pass, and we remember. I was about to embark on an adventure that would lead me to trust my Father God to the max. It is beautiful that for a singer (me), it was a song that became not only life-giving but actually activated my next step with God. I believe that God led me specifically to this song 'Oceans' for what was coming in my life.

Another Life-Changing Song

The next tool the Lord used to woo me back into His Presence was a song from the 'Majesty' CD by Kari Jobe that my mom bought me. The song was 'I Am Not Alone', and when it would come on, I would just cry and cry. I loved the song so much that I made it my mission to get the full piano chords arrangement printed out so I could learn it. With my limited piano skills this was a bold move, but I was very determined. When I want to, one thing I have is the ability to focus.

I spent (what seemed like) countless hours teaching myself to play the piano at a more advanced level. My goal was that one fine day I could sit at the piano and play the song well from start to finish, and be able to concentrate on letting go and worshipping my Savior. A couple of years back my mom purchased Kari Jobe's CD for me and now it is one of my all-time favorites, as well as a safe refuge for me. As I listen the powerful words comfort me. Depending on the situation, I experience comfort and joy in differing ways. More on 'I Am Not Alone' in a moment.

I recommend both CDs by Kari Jobe and Hillsong United. Many of us have to spend a lot of time driving various places. Listen, the Lord is always ready to speak to us, one way or the other.
I suggest that listening to anointed CDs like these two is a great investment of your drive time. And it's not illegal. Like chatting on your Cell Phone is.

Road Trip, Anyone?

Mom called me and invited me to join her on a Road Trip through Beautiful British Columbia and some time by the lake. Mom was scheduled to speak at two churches and free accommodation was offered from our friend Barb. Yep, the same one who confronted me lovingly back in Chapter 4 of this book. She was doing No. 9 on the list above, calling me on trying to be someone I am not, and becoming something of a kaleidoscope in the process. Good old Barb.

Jay and I joined my mom for that week at the lake, which became a time of reflection and reading, and also processing and debate. We were wide open, and many cool things (I call them nuggets) happened during that week. Jay was planning to go fishing one morning and use my Dad's (Roman) old fishing rod, but before he could use it, it needed some repair. Not being from the area, we had asked directions to a place that could possibly fix the rod. We got lost. Then Mom prayed. We found the fishing shop promptly and took it into the store. The owner was there and after hearing our story, he asked to take a look at the rod. He smiled, explained what Roman had done to the rod, and then the owner fixed it right then and there, free of charge. A nugget!

If the Enemy steals from you, it's best to commit that to the Lord, and let Him fight your battles.

An unfortunate event took place and I knew I had to forgive. It is not always easy to forgive when you feel robbed or cheated. This is how I was feeling. To save face I will not go into details here, but those involved know what they did.

As we drove through the beautiful landscape, I should have seen all the mountains, lakes and trees. I was too upset: Mentally wrestling with a range of feelings from self-pity and resentment to anger. All of this seething pain directed at those who hurt me. I had Mom pull the car over at a rest stop so I could get out and stand on a cliff overlooking the lake, and talk to God.

Standing there on the cliff, I screamed at the top of my lungs: 'I surrender all, God!' I didn't feel any better, but I knew that I had to forgive. I said it again: 'I surrender all, God!' And again. Then I just stood there with tears streaming down my cheeks, allowing the sun to dry the tears, while I took in all the beauty around me. It was cathartic, it was necessary and it was good. Just another step in my journey of forgiveness and love.

The Music Comes Back

Time for the next nugget. The next day was Thursday, and at the local restaurant they had an

open mic night. A night on the town, Mom, Jay and me. Dinner and live entertainment. Yay!
When the singing began Mom invited the owners over to talk with us. She mentioned that her daughter here just happened to sing and play the piano. Nice how some people feel free to offer our abilities on the spot, hey? I realize that Mom is just proud of me and likes to show me off, but the fact is I hadn't sang in public for six whole years. That is a considerable chunk of time.

However that wasn't the worst part: I had never played piano in public before. Though usually I am a pretty confident, extroverted performer, I felt a bit nervous in this situation. I smiled and quietly told them that I would think about it and let them know. While we ate, I kept trying to avoid the decision. Then a thought just dropped into my mind: "Kelly, no one here knows you. You can do this." I got up and walked over to the Owners and told them that I would love to play and sing for them that evening. I was about to face my fear front and centre. There was no turning back. What song should I choose?

I selected Kari Jobe's 'I Am Not Alone', an ambitious choice for sure. One: it is a Christian song, and this was a secular venue. Two: it is a slow song, and more uptempo songs usually go over better. Three: I was a beginner on piano. But I shouldn't have been afraid at all, God was with me as I shared his incredible love through the music. He was working in me, and He was working through me. That is about as good as it gets.

Next we went to a beautiful town called Trail, BC. We found a coffee shop just off the highway, and I found another nugget. As I walked in, I was excited to see an old upright piano sitting there, just begging to be played. I asked the Owner if it would be OK for me to play and sing.

He agreed, and liked my material so much that he invited me back every day for as long as we were in town. I was delighted, to have such a great opportunity to practice and play, and to worship in public.

What a great holiday for Mom, Jay and me! Eventually duties at home took Jay back to Calgary, and Mom and I went on to complete her itinerary. At the Church in Trail, Mom asked me to play a couple of songs before she preached. It felt so good, so natural to be back in the saddle again. No matter where it is, there is something about ministering in song that makes me feel at home.
I don't even try to explain it anymore, it just does.

Our final stop (and my next nugget) was in Nelson, BC. I call it "hippy-ville". If we were not committed to our friends and family where we are now, Jay and I could easily make this beautiful place home. I love the easy-going, laid-back feel. I also got to sing and play, ministering to people, after Mom preached. After years of hurt and running, God was steadily rebuilding my soul and confidence once again. Thank you Mom. When is our next road trip?

Affirmations

I want to conclude with a couple of thoughts and a series of affirmations.

1) I did not choose God, He chose me first. At my lowest of lows He called me back to his side and

gave me a safe place to lay my weary head. He loves me enough to never leave me or forsake me. I am so grateful for that.

2)   I want to love others the way that Jesus loves me. Not based on their behaviour or their appearance, but to see beyond that and simply accept them and love them for who they are right now.

Revelation 12:11 `...they triumphed over him by the blood of the Lamb and the word of their testimony...'

3)   No one is born hating someone else just because they are different. No, people learn to hate. The good news is that they can also be taught to love. Love comes more naturally, from the heart. Hate comes from a place of fear. Fear is fed by insignificance and insecurity which in turn breeds envy or jealousy and finally fills the heart with anger and bitterness. How does love handle anger? Love dispels, dissolves and disarms anger. The Bible in 1 John 4:18 says that perfect love casts out fear.

4)   When we feel a sense of acceptance and belonging it is easy to fit in and feel comfortable. Why? 1 John 4:18. Most people will tell you that there is nothing worse than the feeling that everyone is talking negatively about you. It can begin a brutal spiral down into a holy huddle, all by yourself. A 'pitty trip' like that can happen really quickly. Problem is you have no real proof that they are even talking about you at all. It started when fear walked into the room. Fear leads to

doubt, and second guessing. What follows is feeling sorry for yourself. Add in a little anger, and you have your own genuine Pitty Party!

Does this have to happen this way? Of course not. What if you walked into the room and first assessed the crowd. Someone walked up and introduced herself, and then took you around the room introducing you to everyone. What might have been fear is completely disarmed by a small gesture of love and acceptance. One simple act of kindness intercepts hate and replaces it with love.

All You Need Is…

I have facilitated many workshops on conflict resolution. My favourite quote was: '…kill them with kindness.' Why does that work so well, so often? Have you ever tried to stay mad at someone who continues to be nice to you? It's very difficult. (If that is not difficult for you, then I suggest that you might have some serious issues…) Try yelling at your spouse while they are kissing you on the cheek.

A simple but powerful message from a Beatles' song: All you need is love…

Even more powerful is the greatest book on Joy (in the Bible), the book of Philippians. From his own experiences Paul gives us practical ways to find joy. He finds himself in prison, in the sea after a shipwreck, after a beating, he learns and finds joy by adjusting his moments. Just like putting on a new coat, we need to make small adjustments until the fit is just right. Put on your coat of Joy.

Using My Brokenness…

Proverbs 6, talks about taking back what was stolen.

> *The breakthrough is in the brokenness.*
> *The beauty of God comes in hardship.*
> *The gratitude comes in the loss.*
> *The well is filled in the emptiness.*
> *The joy comes in the shifting.*
> *The love comes in the rejection.*

One of the greatest moments you will get with God are the moments of pain that we experience here on earth, because when we get to Heaven we will not be broken, or have pain, sickness or rejection.

It May Sound Crazy, But…

To some of you reading, this will sound absurd. Why should I be thankful for the tough stuff I go through? Celebrating our failures is an opportunity for success. The Bible tells me to, is the other answer. Consistently Paul teaches us to do just the opposite to what the natural man does.

> *'…Be happy (fortunate, to be envied) is the man whose strength is in you, in whose heart are the highways to Zion. Passing through the valley of weeping (Baca), they make it a place of springs; the early rain also fills (the pools) with blessings.*

They go from strength to strength (increasing in victorious power); each of them appears before God in Zion.`

Psalms 84:5-7

Chapter 15: **Journey to the Finish Line**

Two Contrasting World Views

When you look at most advertising, the thinking is that the easier that life is, the better it is. For the most part, this is the prevailing thinking of our age. The goal is one of comfort and ease, along with the elimination of stress, pressure and hardship.

What do we take when we don't feel well? A "pain reliever." Where do we want to live? On "Easy Street." What will give me a better night's rest? A new mattress with better features, of course. When is Life at its best? On a luxury vacation. What can the winner of the lottery achieve? A "life of endless fun, and no pressure."

Back in the 1960s, even the Beatles sang: *"Got a good reason / For taking the easy way out ...."*

There's no doubt about it: our secular society seems to be pre-occupied with making things in life as easy as is possible. This belief system is not only ingrained but being constantly reinforced by a relentless and very obviously secular Media. Compelling as this might seem on the surface, what Jesus teaches, is very different. Jesus teaches that the life of the believer could not be any more different than "life on Easy Street."

I have diligently explained in this book that we are on a journey – a journey to the finish line. The Bible describes two roads: a broad road (leading to Destruction) and a narrow road (leading to Eternal

Life). In stark contrast to the world's view, we know that part of our mission is to go through trials and to endure hardships because this is part of the refining process. It is in these hard times that we are chiseled into a masterpiece. We don't enjoy what it takes to get there; however, with every hardship, another hard surface is chipped away. These qualities that all of us struggle with – such as pride, anger and selfishness – are being chipped away. It is not fun, and it's not easy either.

Not long ago, at my biological father's bedside, I witnessed some of those chipping away moments. In the Western world as a society, we have several protocols and mechanisms. There are definitely things that you simply don't do in mixed company or in public. In the realm of death and dying, many of those agreed upon constraints diminish.

What is left of my biological father's life now depended solely on others. It is rather hard to hold on to personal dignity when we are in a four-bed ward of a hospital, with your backside wide open to the world. My father was used to doing things for himself – but now, like it or not, he must rely on others who are strangers. Bodily functions – such as going to the bathroom – are now announced to the room instead of him slipping quietly away to privacy. Everyone hears his burps and flatulence. No apologies are necessary. A grown man is reduced to being rather like a baby once again. No one is offended, and no one worries about it. Being polite and discreet, these qualities are not important, not in situations like this. There are no fears of rejection. Above all, there is total surrender.

In the Light of Eternity

We human beings spend such a large percentage of our lives, our precious time, trying to please others. When we get to the end of the age, the realization hits us between the eyes: *"For what?"*

Why did we waste our time on such futile pursuits? It certainly was not for our own benefit. In the light of eternity, do practices like these really matter? Is it good for me to stop and take stock of my life? Am I still on track? Am I still pursuing my first love with all my heart?

What are the things that are truly most precious to us? Love, joy and peace! We hold the key to the treasure box. All of us sincerely desire to live life to the fullest, and to live without regret or fear. Then it hits me: the greatest gift is free choice.

Poetry From My Heart and Spirit

(The following is a free-form verse which I am inspired to share with you, dear Reader.)

Peace and Love

Love never gets old, though wrinkled and cold, However spoiled, broken or frail
The heart will live on, no matter how failed, Kicked down or fooled...
The value of love is in the forgiving.

*Love never gets old, peace to calm the soul,
Life to live without regret, lingering or defeat..
Understanding the power of receiving
Forgiveness is passing all understanding
When receiving His Peace & Love.*

*In it all, ups and downs, highs and lows,
Affliction, and adversity, trials or persecution.
In blessing and joy, my most favorite of all is peace.*

He Knows My Name

*Then ultimately Heaven... live forever
young… in my complete form.
Ah, how I long to be with You, my King
Heaven is Eternity.
Spirit first, then body and soul.*

*Why, my Lord, do we stay blind,
choosing these lenses to be tinted
 instead of clear?*

*We want to live forever, but want credit
For getting there. We are so selfish,
God forgive us. Guide us, guide me.
As we desire, so be it.
I choose You.*

*The greatest gift God gives us is choice.
The sacrifice was Jesus Christ, His Son.
We make choices every day
Which determine the rest of our lives
Both here in this journey on Earth, and*

In the next journey in Heaven for Eternity.

The most beautiful of creation in its most Lavishing display. Ah, the canvas I could paint…
I anticipate the Glorious Day when I see You face to face...

When I walk along the shores of the Grand Ocean, sands made of gold beneath my feet...
Oh, what a Glorious Day that will be!

Choice is so powerful: it can make or break, create or take, tear down or build...
Choose wisely, which by the way
When asked for, is offered free.
I am not alone.

Important Thoughts

Throughout our lives, Jay and I are convinced that God has been with us. We have been aware of His presence in the adversity that we have faced, and also in the trials that we have had to endure. We have seen Him in the good times as well, and in our celebrations. God is our Anchor, and He keeps us anchored. It is not a small thing to say that He is our hope.

Simply put, it is our Faith in Jesus Christ directing our path. We have embraced the journey. You can see through my story that, as a family, we have gone through many trials over the years. To use the train metaphor, He has been the Engineer of our train. When we have derailed, He has put us back on the track every time. Though the final destination is the same, Jesus gives us the choice to select our own directions.

I am grateful for the trials in my life, as they have helped make me who I am today, and helped me understand. The tough times have developed us. This is the beautiful result that God intended for us, which He speaks of in Ecclesiastes: *"He makes all things beautiful, in His time."* I know He has a Master Plan for all of us. I have seen Him as the Artist, while I am the canvas. My painting is sometimes black and white; at other times, it is glorious, and full color.

Brokenness

God tells us He does not despise a broken spirit. Being broken is being real. In that "realness," we need to share our journey from an honest place, with the intention of helping others. Being broken is not to gain identity or attention for ourselves. It is in our brokenness that we grow. We let the Holy Spirit come into our hurt. We must be vigilant so that our hurt does not define us and become our identity. We want to bring God into our hurt so that we can be healed. But we don't want to stay there. It is amazing how God works in our lives, even through brokenness.

The Three

We remember Shadrach, Meshach and Abednego, who had their faith in God tested. That was an understatement! It was an extreme situation in public, and lesser people (people less committed to God) may have easily folded under the pressure. These three were so committed and passionate about their faith in God, they literally put it on the line. *"We trust God, and believe He will deliver us. Even if He doesn't, we still trust God, and we will not bow down!"* (Daniel 3:18-20 paraphrased.) The enemy acted quickly and threw the three into the fiery furnace. Shadrach, Meshach and Abednego had hope ... and their God – the only God – came through in spectacular fashion.

Too often this kind of Bible story gets only told in Sunday School. Yes, our children need to know it, but the truth and power of this story goes far beyond just telling children. Please, dear Reader, remember this true story, as it will inspire and help you greatly throughout your life.

A Great Gift From God

One of the greatest gifts God has given to Jay and I happened in Kelowna, British Columbia, a few years ago. We regard this as an epiphany. Both of us received this vision at the same time, and that was amazing. It was sort of like watching a movie wheel clip-by-clip, but in fast motion.

We watched our lives from thirty years ago flash before our eyes. Not only did we see what happened ... but we understood and noticed how God was with us throughout the journey in every circumstance. Many lessons were learned in the stormy times, including His faithfulness. God, the "Nurturer," never leaves or forsakes us.

Brooding

Like a mother hen over her baby chicks, God has hovered over us. This is the nature of God. The first example of God hovering goes back to the very beginning, when God was creating the Earth:

> *In the beginning, God created the Heavens and the Earth. Now the Earth was formless and empty; darkness covered the surface of the watery depths, and the Spirit of God was* **hovering** *over the surface of the waters.*
> Genesis 1:1-2; emphasis added

The word "hovering" is sometimes translated *"brooding,"* which is what birds do on top of eggs. Hens brood on eggs. Like a mother hen, God brooded over the Earth keeping the Earth warm, much like an incubator. This also displays the "mother side of God," as in Isaiah 46:3 and 66:13. The "feminine attributes" of God are those of a mother, or nurturer.

Knowing God's Ways

After all these years and all that we have been through, we still don't fully understand all of God's reasons. Yet we trust that His ways are better than our ways. If we fully understood, then we would not need faith anymore – and the Bible is clear:

"Without faith, it is impossible to please God"
(Hebrews 11:6).

So we have never lost our faith or our hope. We stand strong in Who God says He is, and we always come right to the Father for help. Sometimes people ask me in a whisper: *"Kelly, what is your secret? How do you do it? How do you stay together, considering all you have gone through?"* Good questions!

God is our secret! We have never stopped believing in Jesus Christ and His grace extended to us. We have never forgot Who the Author of our faith is.

Some believe for certain results. We didn't. We simply put our faith into the One to Whom we were praying. As we were nurtured, God showed us His life, making it clear how His hand was there to guide us, train us and walk with us through every step. In a larger sense, I believe that this is the "season of the Nurturer." God is revealing truth by quickening our understanding.

My son, do not forget My teaching, but let your heart keep My commandments; for length of days and years of life and peace will I add to you.
Proverbs 3:1-2

I do not write these things to shame you but to admonish you as my beloved children. For if you were to have countless tutors in Christ, yet you would not have many fathers; for in Christ Jesus, I became your father through the gospel.

1 Corinthians 4:14-15

Our Identity is in Christ, and it is like putting on a coat. The coat covers us, protects us and teaches us. We "wear" Him. When we continue to live out of our hurts and lack, we then become that same thing: hurting and lacking.

We tend to look for people to see us differently because of what we have gone through, and we say: *"Well, sister, you just don't know what I have gone through ...."* No, I don't know what you have gone through because – news flash! – what you have gone through does not (necessarily) make you who you are! What you have done does not define who you are.

Some people feel some sense of entitlement because of what they have been through, and have certain expectations as to how they want to be treated. They take this on as part of their identity.

Have you ever made this statement: *"That isn't fair!* Was the crucifixion fair?

A Dream Come True

I have carried a dream for many years, a dream for women. It is not a secret. I have spoken of it widely, to all my friends and family, and even beyond that. My passion is for women to come into the light of truth and achieve the exploits for God which we were meant to do.

Created in His Image, we are more than just "helpers" – we are leaders, equipped with different gifts than men. Not more than men, not less ... just different. I believe there is a place in God's plan for us to get into the trenches, get our hands dirty and obey our calling. The Nurturer of God, also known as *El Shaddai*: mighty and powerful, and still loving and nourishing.

I have stated that "finding is reserved for the seekers." Recently, God led me to India, where I discovered a mountain of insight into this. While there, I was given the opportunity to be used by God for women. It was powerful. They had me speak to a village of women about value and equality.

I told them how much God loves them, and that He gave His Son for them. Some of them had never heard before that they indeed had value. I spoke of significance, that they were not second- or third-class citizens. I told them they were not some piece of meat, but they had significance.

Remember: this is in India. Because the culture in India is so complicated, I knew that the ladies listening needed to hear they were both loved and accepted. That was my place to begin. What better place for God to allow my dreams to come true than to a group of women who need love and acceptance so much!

Let me leave you with the same quote I gave those women: *"It is not what you will do for God, it is what He will do through you. That is how much value He places on you."* Hebrews 11 has such an encouraging message on faith:

"Now faith is confidence in what we hope for, and the assurance about what we do not see. This is what the Ancients were commended for. By faith, we understand that the Universe was formed at God's command, so that what is seen was not made out of what was visible." Faith is action.

Prayer:

Father, with great expectation, I call forth here on Earth as it is in Heaven, Your great love and nurturing heart over this generation. That we would seek You first, rest in who You are, and trust in Your Love for us. I agree that You, Oh Lord, will encounter this generation with dreams and visions, and an overwhelming awareness of Your Love and Presence. Lord, I pray that peace would blanket our hearts and minds, that wisdom would equip us like arrows, with great precision to deliver us into greater understanding, and liberty to walk out Your Truth and Justice. Teach us how to nurture others as you nurture us. I pray this through your Son Jesus Christ of Nazareth. Amen!

COPYRIGHT & RESOURCES

Page 29: The Merriam-Webster Dictionary. Copyright © 2016 by Merriam-Webster Collegiate; all rights reserved; used with permission.

Page 42: *"His Eye Is On the Sparrow";* copyright © 1905 by Civilla D. Martin (lyrics) and Charles H. Gabriel (composer); Public Domain.

Page 64: Loren Cunningham QUOTATION INFORMATION.

Page 70-71: *"Ten Don'ts to Remember"* Also known as *"A Creed to live by"* by Nancy Sims; copyright © 2016. Used with permission

Page 71: *"Feelings"* by Louis Gasté (Loulou Gasté); copyright © 1974; all rights reserved; used with permission. Performed 1975 by Morris Albert.

Page 84: ARNOLD SKOLNICK description

Page 98: *"This Is Going to Be the Best Day of My Life";* copyright ?; by Aaron Accetta, Zachary Barnett, Shep Goodman, David Rublin, Matthew Sanchez, James Shelley, Michael Goodman; published by Roba Music, Sony/ATV Music Publishing LLC; all rights reserved; used by permission.

Page 107: *"If I Could Turn Back Time";* copyright © 1989 by Diane Warren and Guy Roche; all rights reserved; used with permission. Performed by Cher, *Heart of Stone* album.

Page 151: *"We Need To Hear From You"*; Sandra Crouch © YEAR; publisher information; all rights reserved; used by permission.

Page 195: *"Thank You For Giving to the Lord"* by Ray Boltz.

Page 224: Pharisees/Sadducees (Google)

Page 239: *"Got a good reason / For taking the easy way out"...."* by The Beatles